DEFENCE POLICY-MAKING
A Close-Up View, 1950-1980

A PERSONAL MEMOIR

DEFENCE POLICY-MAKING
A Close-Up View, 1950-1980

A PERSONAL MEMOIR

Sir Arthur Tange

(edited by Peter Edwards)

E PRESS

Published by ANU E Press
The Australian National University
Canberra ACT 0200, Australia
Email: anuepress@anu.edu.au
This title is also available online at: http://epress.anu.edu.au/dpm_citation.html

National Library of Australia
Cataloguing-in-Publication entry

Author: Tange, Arthur, Sir, 1914-2001.
Title: Defence policy-making : a close-up view, 1950-1980 / Sir Arthur Tange ; editor: Peter Edwards.
ISBN: 9781921313851 (pbk.) 9781921313868 (PDF)
Series: Canberra papers on strategy and defence ; 169
Subjects: Tange, Arthur, Sir, 1914-2001.
             Australia. Dept. of Defence--Officials and employees--Biography.
             Civil service--Australia--Biography.
             National security--Australia--History.
             Australia--Military policy--History.
Other Authors/Contributors:
             Edwards, P. G. (Peter Geoffrey), 1945-
Dewey Number: 355.6092

All rights reserved. No part of this publication may be reproduced, stored in a retrieval system or transmitted in any form or by any means, electronic, mechanical, photocopying or otherwise, without the prior permission of the publisher.

The *Canberra Papers on Strategy and Defence* series is a collection of publications arising principally from research undertaken at the SDSC. Canberra Papers have been peer reviewed since 2006. All Canberra Papers are available for sale: visit the SDSC website at <http://rspas.anu.edu.au/sdsc/canberra_papers.php> for abstracts and prices. Electronic copies (in pdf format) of most SDSC Working Papers published since 2002 may be downloaded for free from the SDSC website at <http://rspas.anu.edu.au/sdsc/working_papers.php>. The entire Working Papers series is also available on a 'print on demand' basis.

Strategic and Defence Studies Centre Publications Program Advisory Review Panel: Emeritus Professor Paul Dibb; Professor Desmond Ball; Professor David Horner; Professor Hugh White; Professor William Tow; Professor Anthony Milner; Professor Virginia Hooker; Dr Coral Bell; Dr Pauline Kerr

Strategic and Defence Studies Centre Publications Program Editorial Board: Professor Hugh White; Dr Brendan Taylor; Dr Christian Enemark; Miss Meredith Thatcher (series editor)

Cover design by ANU E Press

© Commonwealth of Australia 2008
Apart from any use as permitted under the Copyright Act 1968 all other rights are reserved.

Contents

Preface vii
    Arthur Tange (1914–2001) viii
    Editorial note x
    Acknowledgements xi
About the Editor xiii

Chapter 1. The Road to Russell 1
    External Affairs 1945 1
    International Security Issues: 1950 and beyond 3
    Defence Management in the 1950s: A view from Canberra 7
    External Affairs and Defence cooperation 10
    The grip of the past in the strategic outlook 11
    America's definition of the ANZUS obligation 12
    Interlude in India 15
    After India: Where to move? 17
    The Defence Department appointment 19
    Defence Minister Fraser: His strategic outlook 20
    The scope of the Defence Group empire 24
    Five Defence Group Ministries: Previous unsuccessful reforms 24
    Managing the Department with limited powers 27
    Fraser's initiatives—and conflicts with Gorton 29
    Gorton the Defence Minister 34
    Fairbairn: Minister for Defence 1971 36
    The Department's 1972 'Defence Review': New ideas 40
    Final months of McMahon's Coalition Government 45

Chapter 2. Labor in Office 49
    Labor's policies 49
    Consultations and plans for merging five Departments 52
    Strategy for making the changes 54
    Abolition of the Service Boards: Reasons 56
    Direct discussion—The Secretary and four Service Chiefs: Conclusions reached 57
    Civilians and Service Officers: Their relative authority 60
    Ministerial acceptance of the Recommendations 62
    Members of Parliament and others: Reactions in Parliament and elsewhere—extent of command power 63
    Some objectives not achieved 65
    Interim arrangements—changes needed in the Department 67
    Managing the Department—The 1973 political environment ... 68
    Disclosure of the American presence—Conflict with Labor Left 69
    The Joint US–Australian Defence Facilities 71

Limited disclosure on Pine Gap and Nurrungar 74
Labor's problem with the North West Cape Naval Communications
Station 76
The Lloyd affair—Barnard's rebuke of Tange 77
Redefining the threat basis for Defence planning 79
Barnard's negotiations with Washington 83
Other decisions for Barnard 85
New problems for the Defence Department under Labor 86
Reshaping the force structure under Barnard 88
The Darwin cyclone 90
A retrospect on Barnard 91
Whitlam's Royal Commission: Enquiry into Intelligence Services 92
Reflections looking back: Whitlam and the Central Intelligence
Agency 94
The 1975 changes: A new Minister, Chiefs of Staff and 'the
Dismissal' 96

Chapter 3. The Early Fraser Ministry 99
James Killen, Minister for Defence 99
Problems to overcome in the new system 100
Public perceptions in the politics of Defence 102
Differing views on our strategic interests 103
President Carter and the Indian Ocean 105
Inflation: Its consequences for Defence in the 1970s 106
Differences with the Royal Commission on Intelligence 108
Experiences serving Malcolm Fraser 112
A refuge in the mountains 115
The Defence Science Laboratories: Management 117
Planning the Defence Force Academy: Obstacles 119
Using soldiers in support of police 122
Final months in the Department 124
The gap between the strategic guidance and Defence
preparations 124
Personnel policies and practices in the Services 126
Defamatory media fabrications 127
Post retirement experiences 129
On serving Ministers 130
Reflections on a personal journey 138
Bibliography 141
Index 143

Preface

Sir Arthur Tange was perhaps the most powerful Secretary of the Australian Defence Department and one of the most powerful of the great 'mandarins' who dominated the Commonwealth Public Service between the 1940s and the 1970s. Here 'powerful' means having a strong, and often decisive, influence on both administration and policy. Tange exerted that influence by virtue of his intellectual capacity, his administrative ability and the sheer force of his personality. He served as Secretary of the Defence Department from 1970 to 1979, the last decade of his career, having previously served as Secretary of the Department of External Affairs (later renamed Foreign Affairs) from 1954 to 1965.

Tange wrote this account in his last years. The last draft was dated 6 November 2000, about six months before his death on 10 May 2001 at the age of 86. It is a memoir rather than an autobiography, being based largely on memory supplemented by limited reference to documentary material. He worked on it in his home in the Canberra suburb of Manuka, tapping at an ageing typewriter on his dining-room table, while I was working in his study on a full-length biography. That biography, *Arthur Tange: Last of the Mandarins* (Allen & Unwin, 2006), made use of this text as well as his personal papers (now held in the National Library of Australia as MS9847) and other documentary and oral sources.

While that book gives a full account of his life, many friends, family members and former colleagues wanted to see his own account. Controversies from his time in Defence, including those associated with 'the Tange report' and 'the Tange reforms', echo to this day, and it is still easy to identify both staunch admirers and vitriolic critics in defence and public service circles.

This memoir says little about Tange's life and career before he came to Defence in 1970. He intended to write a similar memoir of his time in External Affairs, but only a few preliminary passages had been sketched by the time of his death. Nevertheless, one of the major themes implicit in this memoir (and argued in greater detail in the biography) is the extent to which his administrative decisions and policy advice in Defence in the 1970s were based on his experience in External Affairs in the 1950s and 1960s. As Secretary of External Affairs, for example, he was a member of the Defence Committee, the most important source of advice to the Government on defence policy. Through that and other associations, Tange had a close view of the relevant Ministers and their most senior advisers, uniformed and civilian. This account shows what lessons he derived from that experience and how he applied those lessons when he, rather unexpectedly, became Secretary of the Defence Department.

Arthur Tange (1914–2001)

Arthur Harold Tange was born in Sydney on 18 August 1914. His father, Charles Louis Tange, was a lawyer who moved from Sydney to an orchard property at Mangrove Mountain, near Gosford on the Central Coast of New South Wales. This proved a rash investment, losing the family much of the financial and social status that had been gained by Charles's father, Anton Tange, who had emigrated from Denmark in 1854. Although he was the seventh and youngest child of his father's two marriages, Arthur's upbringing was in many ways more like that of an only child. He attended Woy Woy Primary School and Gosford High School, matriculating with good results although aged only 16. With the Depression starting, Arthur was fortunate to get a job with the Bank of New South Wales, of which the General Manager (the position today known as the Chief Executive Officer of Westpac) was Sir Alfred Davidson, who was married to Arthur's oldest half-sister. Davidson's support not only secured Arthur a job, but also enabled him to go to university. He studied arts, majoring in economics, at the University of Western Australia (UWA). Arthur took an honours degree, then regarded as a post-graduate qualification, writing a thesis on the Australian banking system. In later life Arthur liked to speak of the three great achievements of his student days in Perth: he gained a first-class honours degree; he played rugby for Western Australia against the Springboks; and he won the hand of Marjorie Shann, daughter of the UWA professor of economics and history, Edward Shann. Arthur and Marjorie were married at Christ Church, Claremont, on 19 November 1940. They subsequently had two children, Christopher John, born in Canberra on 7 April 1944, and Jennifer Jane, born in New York on 31 January 1947.

The Bank of New South Wales employed Arthur first in the Economic Department, the bank's think tank in Sydney, and then in Fiji. After the outbreak of war in 1939 he was protected under the manpower regulations from being called up for military service, but in 1942 he was recruited, as a temporary research officer, to the Department of Labour and National Service. His division soon became the Department of Post-War Reconstruction (DPWR), in which Arthur spent much of his time working on the international negotiations, principally with the United States and the United Kingdom, over the Lend-Lease agreement. In 1944 he was a member of the small Australian delegation to the international conference at Bretton Woods, which established the International Monetary Fund and the World Bank.

Towards the end of the 1939–45 war, the Department of External Affairs (DEA) developed an interest in economic aspects of international affairs. For some months Tange's services were shared between DPWR and External Affairs, until in 1946 he joined the DEA full-time. He was immediately posted to the Australian Mission to the United Nations in New York, where his colleagues included one of his future Ministers, Paul Hasluck. On his return to Canberra, he rose quickly to a senior position in the small and youthful External Affairs. In 1953, Tange was sent to the Australian Embassy in Washington, with the diplomatic rank of Minister. The Government probably hoped that, as deputy head of mission, he would curb the tendency of the Ambassador, Sir Percy Spender, to act as if he were still the Minister for External Affairs. This task, however, proved too much for Tange.

Within a year, the Minister for External Affairs, R.G. Casey (later Lord Casey), offered Tange the position of Secretary of his Department. Tange took up the post in early 1954, aged 39. Over the next eleven years he proved a strong leader, reforming and modernising many aspects of the Department's administration and greatly improving its ability to give the Government well-informed advice on foreign policy. Within weeks of his taking up the post, External Affairs had to handle the breach in relations with the Soviet Union occasioned by the Petrov affair. The subsequent years saw considerable growth in the Department's capacity to represent Australia abroad, especially in Asia, and to advise the Government. There were also numerous international crises, including those associated with Suez, Laos, West New Guinea, Indonesia and Malaysia, and Vietnam. In some cases Tange was at the heart of Australian policy-making; in others, most notably the Australian commitment to Vietnam in 1964–65, he appears to have been deliberately excluded from influence.

This partly reflected his changing relationship with his Ministers, who were four of the most significant politicians of the twentieth century: Casey, Robert Menzies, Garfield Barwick and Paul Hasluck. Tange had an almost filial relationship with Casey and a close and effective working relationship with Barwick. Menzies' attitude towards Tange seems to have been adversely affected during the two years that Menzies was Minister for External Affairs as well as Prime Minister (1960–61), but the chilliest relationship was with his former colleague in New York, Hasluck.

Tange was knighted in 1959, the year he turned 45, and from then on was almost invariably known as 'Sir Arthur'. He had previously been made an Officer of the Order of the British Empire (OBE) in 1953 and Commander in the same order (CBE) in 1955. Later, after the introduction of an Australian honours system, he was made a Companion of the Order of Australia (AC) in 1977.

In 1965 Tange was dispatched as High Commissioner to India, the only head-of-mission appointment in his diplomatic career. There he remained for five years, often thinking that he would never be offered another ambassadorial or other senior appointment. Then, in late 1969, he was successively offered, in circumstances that mingled weighty decisions with farce, the three most important positions open to an official working in national security: those of ambassador in Washington, Secretary of the Defence Department, and his former post as Secretary of External Affairs. Although he had started preparing himself for Washington, he turned that option aside in order to become Secretary of Defence.

Tange served there from early 1970 until his retirement at the time of his 65th birthday in August 1979. This period included two changes of government, from the conservative coalition to Labor and back to the coalition. The Prime Ministers and Ministers for Defence whom he served included John Gorton and Malcolm Fraser in both capacities, as well as William McMahon, David Fairbairn, Gough Whitlam, Lance Barnard, William Morrison, and James Killen. These were years of major, often controversial, reform in the administration of Defence, which at times brought Tange to public attention. His report on the reorganisation of the Defence group of departments, generally known as 'the Tange report', charted the way for the Departments of Navy, Army, Air and Supply to be merged into the Department of Defence, a process often known as 'the Tange reforms'. These administrative reforms were closely linked to changing ideas on strategic policy, including the relative importance of alliance commitments and developments in Australia's immediate neighbourhood in the shaping of Australian defence policy.

This memoir is Tange's own account of his part in those administrative reforms and policy shifts. It also records his involvement—or non-involvement or alleged involvement—in several of the political crises of the 1970s, including the downfall of John Gorton as Prime Minister and the dismissal of the Whitlam Government.

The memoir closes with some brief comments on events in his retirement and reflections on his life and career, especially his relations with many ministers and Prime Ministers. Sir Arthur Tange died on 10 May 2001. His funeral service was private, but a State Memorial service was held in Parliament House, Canberra, on 24 May 2001.

Editorial note

This memoir was written very late in Sir Arthur Tange's long life. Earlier in his retirement, he had written a short family history, entitled *Looking Back*, which was perhaps a better example of his skill as a writer. Tange was always fond of writing but recognised that, throughout his life, he was inclined to be prolix and to insert too many qualifying phrases into a single sentence. Some errors found their way into the text, some no doubt occasioned by the difficulty of reading his typescript with its many handwritten annotations and amendments. Several individuals were identified only by surnames, and he was not always consistent in spelling terms such as 'South East Asia' and 'Southeast Asia'.

In editing the text, I have kept editorial interventions to the minimum. In a few cases, I have adjusted the word order, punctuation and/or syntax to make the meaning clear, but have restricted that practice to the occasions when it seemed absolutely necessary. Where appropriate I have added forenames and positions. Footnotes have been added where they seemed necessary, including those cases where Tange had specifically indicated that he wanted sources to be noted. References to other relevant works have been made where that seemed especially appropriate, but not to the above-mentioned biography, as such references would have appeared on almost every paragraph. Readers should assume that this memoir will be of greatest value if read in close coordination with the relevant passages of the biography.

Throughout, I have sought to preserve not only the meaning but also the style and tone of Tange's text. For example, Tange's use of capital letters for words such as 'Service', 'Department' and 'Minister' have been left unchanged, as a reminder that these are the words of someone who had followed Public Service conventions for several decades.

Acknowledgements

Work on this memoir was carried out in parallel with the research and writing of *Arthur Tange: Last of the Mandarins*. Accordingly, most of the acknowledgements made in the Preface to that work apply here. It is particularly appropriate to record my thanks to the Department of Defence, especially the former Deputy Secretary (and now Professor of Strategic Studies at The Australian National University), Hugh White; to the successive Secretaries of the Department, especially Dr Allan Hawke and Mr Ric Smith; and the heads and members of the Strategic Policy Branch, especially Mr Peter Jennings and Mr Murray Perks.

Generous support from the Pratt Foundation, through its chief executive Mr Sam Lipski, enabled Tange's typescript of this memoir, with its many handwritten annotations and amendments, to be turned into an electronic document.

Mr Christopher Tange and Mrs Jennifer Moir (*née* Tange) provided constant support and encouragement in bringing to the public their father's record. Many colleagues and friends were similarly supportive, with particular thanks being due to Deakin University and the University of New South Wales at the Australian Defence Force Academy, in both of which institutions I held honorary professorships. My wife, Jacky Abbott, has nobly tolerated the presence of Arthur Tange in our life for many years. For a full list of those who have assisted and supported me on the three-part Tange project (writing the biography, editing this memoir, and organising and listing Tange's papers for the National Library of Australia), please see the Preface to the biography.

About the Editor

Peter Edwards is a consultant historian and writer who has published on Australian defence and foreign policies for more than thirty years. He is the official historian of Australia's involvement in Southeast Asian conflicts 1948–75 (Malaya, Borneo and Vietnam), for which he wrote the volumes dealing with strategy and diplomacy, *Crises and Commitments* (1992) and *A Nation at War* (1997). He was made a Member of the Order of Australia (AM) for this work. His most recent book is *Arthur Tange: Last of the Mandarins* (2006). Both *A Nation at War* and *Arthur Tange* won major literary awards.

Dr Edwards is also the author of *Permanent Friends? Historical Reflections on the Australian–American Alliance* (2005), and *Prime Ministers and Diplomats* (1983); the co-editor of *Facing North* (vol. 2, 2003); the editor of *Australia Through American Eyes* (1977); and one of the founding editors of the series of *Documents on Australian Foreign Policy*. He is a former editor, and now a contributing editor, of the *Australian Journal of International Affairs*. Currently Dr Edwards is an honorary Visiting Professor of the University of New South Wales at the Australian Defence Force Academy, Canberra. He has held a number of consultancies with universities and government agencies and is a member of historical advisory committees in the Department of Defence and the Department of Foreign Affairs and Trade.

Chapter 1

The Road to Russell

A career in the Public Service which closed after a decade as Secretary to the Department of Defence started from what might seem an unlikely origin. In 1942, aged 28, I was brought to Canberra from a wartime reserved occupation to work on analysing Australia's interests in the international economic and financial regulations being proposed for Australia's responses by the British and American planners who were preparing for a better world system after the war had been won. For a short period I was made responsible to Dr Roland Wilson (later Secretary to the Treasury), but in 1943 the Labor Government created the Department of Post-War Reconstruction, with J.B. Chifley as its Minister (and concurrently Treasurer) and Dr H.C. 'Nugget' Coombs as its Director-General. I worked under Coombs for several years, preparing papers and advice for several of Australia's most senior economists on the problems to be expected, and the safeguards needed, to protect Australia in the impact of these post-war plans of the two major economic powers. Over the years, I attended several international conferences arranged to discuss and to amend and endorse these plans, beginning with the 1944 Bretton Woods International Monetary Conference.

External Affairs 1945

I was seconded into the Department of External Affairs in 1945. That Department, under the urging of Dr J.W. Burton, was seeking a role in policy in these economic fields, particularly with the prospect of the United Nations and other institutions being set up with various regulatory powers. Apart from Burton, the Department was devoid of experience in economic matters. My secondment became a continuing one, leading to permanence from 1946 onwards.

I have written about my External Affairs years elsewhere.[1] I am here recording only how my interest in national security and defence matters developed. It was that interest that led me to accept, two decades later, the offer by the Gorton/Fraser Ministry[2] to become Secretary to the Department of Defence.

But before this my duties lay elsewhere. I became an international conference handyman and draftsman between 1945 and 1948, based in New York and attending, as adviser and occasionally as leader of delegation, a frenzied round of meetings at which Minister for External Affairs Dr H.V. Evatt's policies of pushing Australia into all the burgeoning specialised international institutions required representation. I had a part in drafting what went into the constitution and the rules of several of the new institutions being established. Returning to the Department in late 1948 from the UN Mission in New York, I was made responsible for overseeing the development of Australian policies and representation in these areas as well as helping formulate our policies in the political organs of the United Nations.

After the Liberal–Country Party Coalition won the 1949 election, I had my first meeting with the new Minister for External Affairs, P.C. Spender. In his Sydney office, a pinkish, shortish man with a bristling moustache greeted me by first denouncing the policies of Evatt that I had been serving and then saying: 'Burton says you know something about economics'. I confessed that I thought I did. He then bade me produce some ideas for him to use at the meeting of British Commonwealth Foreign Ministers scheduled shortly for Colombo. He took me, along with others, to this meeting, and to subsequent meetings to set up the Colombo Plan.

Burton chose to retire in 1951. Spender (after consulting Paul Hasluck, as the latter told me much later) appointed A.S. Watt to succeed him. Hasluck also told me that he had given Spender my name 'in case he wanted a younger man'. Watt was a scholarly man, with experience in the Department, a former Rhodes Scholar and judge's associate whose conservative views would not have commended him to Evatt. He had been sent to serve in Moscow in 1947. Watt retained me on my current duties.

Although not directly involved, I was able to observe the efforts to remedy the distrust and some antagonism that had developed between the Defence Department in Melbourne under Sir Frederick Shedden, and External Affairs under Burton. Watt had served in Washington. He had a deep concern about communism spreading internationally. He had then, and as I observed in later years, a continuing anxiety about the possibility of espionage being directed against officers of the Department, and the security of its communications.

I had been serving overseas between 1945 and late 1948, which were the years of developing differences between Burton and Shedden that several historians have documented.[3] Knowing Burton well, and observing Shedden, I came to believe in later years that the differences were the product of many things: age, education, respect for conventional Public Service practices; but particularly fundamental differences on the issues in East-West relations, on the policy of non-alignment by emerging ex-colonies, and related questions. There was also the competition between a well rooted, if conservative and somewhat complacent, Department and a small group of untried newcomers in Canberra elevated into influence by a radical Labor leadership. Shedden had earned a high reputation by the support he had given Prime Minister John Curtin during the war. He had been committed to collective British Commonwealth defence under British leadership and responsive to the British desire for Australia to make resistance to any Soviet incursion to the Middle East our priority in war—although then and later he was vigilant in preserving Australian authority over its own forces. When I came to know Shedden later, it was not in his best years. I saw little intellectual questioning of strategic priorities, while he attached unusual importance to preserving his personal contacts with the significant wartime figures with whom he had dealt in the past. He was an industrious administrator, rigid in his attachment to procedures, and a skilled defender of turf. In contrast was Burton's belief that international relations should be based on principles rather than power as he would argue—with great self-assurance about the validity of his convictions—calling for conciliation with the Soviet Union, more Australian concern with Southeast Asia, and wariness about a future threat from China. In retrospect I thought conflict between Shedden and the young nonconformist radical was inevitable. There were frictions over practical matters, such as opposition to Shedden's reform of his intelligence apparatus, and Burton's insouciance over evidence of the passage of sensitive information clandestinely to the Soviet Union from one corner of External Affairs.[4]

International Security Issues: 1950 and beyond

In the second half of 1950 the focus of my work underwent a big change, precipitated by North Korea's military invasion of the South. My advisory role was no longer concerned primarily with the economic organs of the United Nations and the new Colombo Plan for aid in Southeast Asia. Spender and Watt now looked to my division to advise on the political and constitutional objectives for the military intervention in defence of South Korea to be laid down in the United Nations and advocated through diplomatic channels. I was drawn into helping to define a security policy for Australia that satisfied several interests—domestic, political, and diplomatic—in relations with the Americans and within the British Commonwealth. They were not easy to reconcile within the framework of the UN approval that was required for the UN campaign. There were sceptics in the non-aligned world about the validity of Western intervention in an Asian country; and when the Communist Chinese entered the war (or when that seemed a possibility to be avoided), disagreement spread over such questions as the admission of Peking [Beijing] to the Chinese seat in the UN Security Council, and whether Peking's claims on Taiwan against Chiang Kai-shek [Jiang Jieshi] should be resisted militarily. On these matters there were Anglo-American disagreements and hardline opinion in the United States. In Australia, particularly after China entered the war, Spender chose to argue against offering political rewards to aggressors, an attitude having wide support as memories of pre-war fascism in Europe exerted their influence. And Spender's supreme objective was to earn agreement from the United States to give him a security treaty, an enterprise in which he had no support from Britain.

The work undertaken by myself and others in this tangle of interests is included in Robert O'Neill's official history[5] and need not be repeated here. But it may be of interest to record some of the ideas which influenced me in tracing my eventual passage into work on Australia's military capabilities as a Pacific nation, with its strategic interest centred on its near neighbourhood rather than Europe, the Middle East or North Asia.

In 1950 we went militarily into North Asia with Australian ground forces. This was a high policy decision fathered by Spender who pushed it through, past what I believe to have been somewhat bewildered colleagues, while fortuitously his cautious Prime Minister, R.G. Menzies, was abroad and unable to take part. Once the decision was made, I advocated, unsuccessfully, that we make a larger military contribution. It was not that I saw any reason for Australian sacrifices to protect the Korean people, governed by a corrupt leader; nor did I see much evidence of spontaneous popular sympathy for this remote people. But our membership of the UN Commission for the Unification of Korea, which Evatt had sponsored and where we were represented by the highly regarded James Plimsoll, gave us a moral as well as a practical duty to come to the aid of the South.

Moreover, preservation of the possibility of a new collective security being founded, we hoped, on the United States had to be fostered. But it should not be at the price, as I saw it, of Australia being dragged into a new distant conflict of dubious merit. I hoped the Government would accept advice not to commit itself to a long-term commitment to give military support to whatever government might emerge in Korea after the North Korean Army had been quelled. In particular I was moved by believing then, and also in subsequent years of crisis in the Western Pacific, that the Government of mainland China should not be provoked into war that could spread into Southeast Asia and the approaches to Australia. I took this view when, with a final peace in Korea yet to be settled, the French were overrun by nationalist forces in Indo-China. While the negotiations for an armistice in Korea were not succeeding, we also had to express attitudes, in New York and Washington, on the activities of General Douglas MacArthur in his free interpretation of his political instructions.

Spender took me to London in early 1951 as he carried his energetic and single-minded campaign to a sceptical British audience. I recall the visit as one of the most determined forays of its kind that I have witnessed. Meetings and public addresses were packed into a few days, before he went on to Washington to take a very important opportunity to put his case for a security treaty direct to President Harry Truman. He left me behind in London, entrusted with the task of composing a telegram to Menzies ranging widely (and somewhat indeterminately) over all the issues.

If historians, when making their meticulous interpretations of what they read, knew how some papers originated, it might lighten their days (and their prose). On his journey to Southampton to join the RMS *Queen Mary*, Spender sat me in the 'dickey seat' of his Daimler to record his thoughts and his instructions. His staccato speech seemed, as always, to be in a race with the agility of his mind. We wound through the villages of southern England cloaked in darkness, except when lights, apparently relics of the Second World War, sporadically illuminated the moving vehicle. They proved essential for making crude handwritten notes. At our destination we parted company in his cabin after he gave me his second thoughts (Spender was not a man of few words), interrupted by an altercation with a majestically uniformed purser upon whom Spender vented his displeasure at the inadequacy of the cabin that Cunard had provided to the Foreign Minister of Australia.

In London I pieced together what I thought Spender had told me to say. The telegram to Canberra is now a small piece in the published history of the times[6] and I doubt that Spender ever saw what he is recorded as saying to his Prime Minster. I had anxieties in those days, but I also had fun.

In the 1950s the Secretary of the Department of External Affairs had no role in decisions on the development of the three arms of the defence force. But when it came to their deployment, membership of the Defence Committee, and advisory sessions with Ministers from time to time, enabled the External Affairs Secretary to express his judgement on where they should not be deployed. It is not possible to say how much influence we had of this kind; for example, in opposing military support to the Dutch in West New Guinea, or in advising the Government to argue the Americans out of defending the off-shore islands in support of Chiang Kai-shek against attacks from the mainland. In the final days of the attempts to settle peace terms for the conflict with China over Korea (and over the issue of repatriation of prisoners of war), we in External Affairs were wary of an American idea of a pledge by the allies in Korea, declared to China, to take punitive action if China broke the negotiated agreements. Widening the war was one of our fears during those years.

These examples of the interconnected interests of External Affairs and Defence illustrate why over some 30 years I held to the view that administrative and inter-Ministerial arrangements were essential to make possible a consensus on security policy. Contrary to the conventional thought that it was only a matter of restraining unwise military initiatives, I came in later years to believe that restraint was needed on the temptation, particularly for Prime Ministers, to inflate Australia's influence in the world, making commitments that outran the community's willingness to provide the resources needed by the Defence Force if Australia's military capability were put to the test.

In mid-1951 R.G. (later Lord) Casey replaced Spender, who had chosen to become Ambassador to the United States. Casey took me on several overseas missions. Those to Southeast Asia reflected his interest in the progress of the British military commanders in Malaya and Singapore in subduing the jungle insurgency. He also wanted to meet and form an impression of the emerging indigenous political leaders. I also accompanied him on a later tour through Cairo and several European capitals, when he led the delegation to the UN General Assembly in Paris. Casey was dismayed by the acrimony of the political debates and by the ferocity of the attacks of Andrei Vyshinsky, the Soviet delegate, on the Western alliance.

When I returned to Canberra in early 1952 I was again advising on the efforts to break the conflict between voluntary and compulsory repatriation of prisoners of war, in order to reach a settlement with the Chinese for an armistice in Korea. At year's end I was appointed to the embassy in Washington, with the rank of Minister, under Spender, in order to pursue this and other matters. I was Australia's liaison officer with senior officers of the US State Department consulting the 16 force contributors in Korea. One of the unrecorded duties that I was given was to exercise restraint on Spender in his free-running presentation of views, often at odds with those of Casey and Watt, on such matters as the Korean negotiations, Indonesia and Dutch New Guinea.

My assignment was cut short when Casey, on a visit to Washington, told me of Watt's desire for a post in Southeast Asia, and offered me appointment as Secretary of the Department. After 12 months in our new home, I packed up my family again, disrupting the children's schooling,[7] and returned to Canberra to take up my new post in January 1954.

While in Washington I saw at first hand the way the Defence Department handled defence relations with the Americans—through a military mission not integrated into the embassy and one senior officer in the embassy. Beyond attending to routine business concerning relations between the armed Services of the two countries, there seemed to be little interest in reporting the defence policies of the United States towards Asia and the vigorous public debates in Congress and elsewhere which had a part in shaping them. Nor was there much evidence of guidance from Melbourne on this subject. Then, and later in Canberra, I wondered whether there was a reluctance to grant Casey leadership in security diplomacy or, more simply, slowness in recognising the implications of the 1951 ANZUS Treaty.

In my new post in Canberra I was propelled by the events of 1954 into helping the Government to respond to the recurring crises in the Western Pacific. The Government sought to attract US involvement for the first time in arresting the spread of communist influence on the Southeast Asian mainland, following the collapse of the French in Indo-China. Support for the legitimacy of the Saigon Government was needed after acceptable terms could not be reached with the communist north for unification of Vietnam in the Geneva Conference. It was a year in which effective cooperation with the Department of Defence on the deteriorating situation to our north had a renewed urgency. Steps were needed to overcome the obstacles to quick and effective cooperation.

Defence Management in the 1950s: A view from Canberra

My first attendance at the Defence Committee had been in 1952. I had then detected some condescension on the part of the Service Chiefs towards my Department. Perhaps this was understandable in the case of Vice-Admiral Sir John Collins and Lieutenant General Sir Sydney Rowell, both lately returned from distinguished service in a great war. The third was a seconded British officer.

The six Departments in the Defence Group (Defence, Navy, Army, Air, Supply, and Defence Support) were under overall policy guidance that seemed to value precedent and procedure over analysis and new thinking. I should acknowledge that there was much management activity in the Defence Group of which External Affairs was necessarily uninformed. We would not have been competent, in any case, to judge whether Defence decisions on manpower and weapons selection, for example, were cost-effective. Our view was confined to the way in which judgements were reached on where these capabilities might have to be deployed—in short, the strategic posture of the country.

The devotion to orderly procedures was symbolised in the mechanistic description used by Shedden to describe the senior policy-making bodies—the 'Higher Defence Machinery'. The staff of the Defence Department was largely civilian, while uniformed Service officers, with the aid of a Departmental Secretary, managed the Services under their respective Ministers. It seemed to us in Canberra that the Defence Department personnel were a mixture of a handful of questioning and perceptive officers and a larger number performing the modest role of guiding Service officers through the unfamiliar terrain of public accountability. This put a premium on providing support to others carrying higher authority, for example as Secretaries to inter-Service committees; guiding but not initiating. Initiative seemed to lie with the Services, or took the form of proposals made to Australia by Britain as the leader of Commonwealth defence planning in the early post-war years.

Decisions by, or offers of consultation from, London or Washington required speedy comprehension of international events and assessment of Australia's interests. The Australian Government sometimes demanded to be consulted simply as a demonstration of our independence. I think that our inability to come up with a reply must have shaken patience in London and Washington on occasions. There was exasperation in Canberra at the necessity to consult the Melbourne 'machinery' when secure communication was difficult, and travel to meetings slow. The Joint Intelligence Committee, unlike its counterpart in London, suffered these disadvantages and was a cumbersome way of drawing conclusions that could be used in a timely way by the Department of External Affairs and by Ministers. The Joint Planning Committee, charged with advising on the feasibility of military operations, was impenetrable by External Affairs. If the Government was to be warned of the need for restraint on a proposed military action, the Committee's advice would have to be challenged later. On one occasion when one of our officers was invited to attend, he heard a cry of alarm from the naval member (later a Rear Admiral): 'There is a stranger in the room'. The Shedden discipline required that all past findings on a subject be laid one upon the other, with consistency valued above innovation. There was much turgid prose. More objective critics than I, in the person of successive official historians, have described the inadequacies of the system.[8]

Both Departments suffered from the remoteness of Ministers from their Departments and from each other. Casey preferred to spend as much time as possible in Melbourne or his country property at Berwick. Other Ministers in the Defence Group were scattered around the continent when Parliament was in recess. Defence Minister Sir Philip McBride, with whom I had much to do in later years when he was Acting Minister for External Affairs, might be beyond reach for one or two days while touring the vast expanse of his sheep runs across the north of South Australia. One ruminated fruitlessly on the ease of consultation among Departments and Ministers in cosy Britain.

Prime Minister Robert Menzies was the pillar to whom we turned when crises demanded a prompt response. He was resident in Canberra and sought the advice of officials methodically, and of relevant Ministers when they were available to meet with him. When Parliament was sitting, these meetings occurred not in Cabinet sub-committees but around Menzies' desk, often late at night. Generally the Ministers for Defence and External Affairs would be present along with the Secretaries of the Prime Minister's and External Affairs Departments, but seldom the Secretary of Defence or a Service Chief because of their isolation in Melbourne. The decisions reached have to be discerned by historians from outgoing telegrams to our missions abroad or to other governments.

When writing in later years of his Cabinet experience, Sir Paul Hasluck remarked on the failure of a Cabinet committee, of which he was a member, to meet and be informed by External Affairs. The comment accompanied some disparaging references to one of his predecessors as Minister for External Affairs, Casey, and was perhaps designed to fortify his criticism of the management of affairs while he was sidelined in the Territories portfolio. Hasluck was apparently unaware of Menzies' preference for *ad hoc* meetings of the kind I have described. Menzies had no disposition for attending Cabinet committee meetings simply for educational purposes.

In my discussions with Shedden over the years I heard few opinions on Australia's strategic interests or priorities. He was more interested, it seemed, in procedures and in respect for the Defence Committee. Absence from its meetings would earn a mild rebuke. His conversation in moments of relaxation, as previously noted, dwelt very much on the famous wartime personalities with whom he had dealt as the adviser and Secretary to Curtin's War Cabinet. I was aware that in that role he had earned the highest respect from the Government. But I found his methods in respect of our strategic interests and their priorities to be unsuited to the new age. Australia was forging a foreign policy in alliance with a new ally and was actively engaged with military situations, rather than directing its attention to British concerns with the Soviet threat in the Middle East. Assessing the strength of potential threats to Australia's independent interests, within the area covered by the ANZUS Treaty, made considerable demands on such intellectual resources as the two Departments possessed. In his dealings with the British, Shedden was vigilant to protect Australia's control of its forces. There was much that needed high-level discussion of issues. But the Defence Committee method looked to subordinate Service officers to come up with recommendations for the Defence Committee to approve or disapprove. The Committee was a place for decision rather than discussion of the substance. I found this hard to resist because it seemed to reflect a use of staff officers in the command system to which the Service Chiefs were attuned, and I was not.

The *Macquarie Dictionary* defines a bureaucrat as 'an official who works by fixed routine without exercising intelligent judgement'. There was an element of such a bureaucrat in Shedden during his final service years.

Shedden seldom appeared in Canberra. I was ready to respect the responsibilities and military knowledge resident in the Defence organisation. Because of this, in August 1954 only six months after becoming Secretary, I wrote to Shedden to ask for his cooperation. It was a time of recurring crises in Asia, and Australia faced the possibility of being drawn into war in support of the Americans. In plain language I had pointed out that errors of judgement by the Americans demanded that we put our views to the Americans promptly as events developed. This would have to be without the benefit of Defence advice if their methods precluded prompt responses to my urgent requests. I recall no response from Shedden or change in his methods. It was a case of priority being given to process rather than to the substance and the outcome.

In the mid-1950s Menzies and his Ministers became dissatisfied with what was coming out of Melbourne. They exerted pressure on Shedden to stand aside and write up his experiences, for which he was given official assistance. It was sad, but presumably a more dignified ending for his career could not be found.

His replacement in 1956 was Edwin (later Sir Edwin) Hicks, formerly Secretary to the Department of Air. His experience lay less in security policy than in the application of organisation and methods to Departments.

External Affairs and Defence cooperation

Slowly the External Affairs and Defence Departments worked more closely together. In 1957 the Secretary of External Affairs was made a full, as distinct from an invited, member of the Defence Committee. This was also the year that the Secretary of the Prime Minister's Department (then Allen Brown) joined the Committee, which was to have consequences for External Affairs authority in later years. External Affairs assumed chairmanship of the Joint Intelligence Committee, recognising it as the prime source of political intelligence, while the Joint Intelligence Bureau in Melbourne assembled military intelligence of a static kind. Preparation of material for meetings of the ANZUS and Southeast Asia Treaty Organisation Councils necessitated joint work, although some continuing problems remained in ensuring that the conclusions of meetings of the military Chiefs in these organisations were presented in a useful way to the External Affairs Minister for his Council meetings. I earlier described the external security situations that demanded joint appreciations between the diplomatic and defence arms of government. As the decade progressed, the growth of the PKI (Partai Komunis Indonesia, the Communist Party of Indonesia) and the growing bellicosity of Indonesia's President Sukarno in respect of Dutch New Guinea and, later, the 'Confrontation' challenge to the birth of Malaysia, required many meetings of the Defence Committee in response to calls on it from Ministers. Beyond all this was the dangerous escalation of the confrontation between the nuclear powers, on which the Committee offered the best judgement it could on the information given us. While some academics offered analytical judgement on the effectiveness or otherwise of deterrence of the Soviet Union, I do not think the Australian Ministers were equipped to understand the complexities of the issues. Nor do I believe that any Australian position other than an offer of diplomatic support would have weighed with the United States.

Through the Defence Committee I made many associations and some lasting friendships with the top levels of the Services and with their British, American and New Zealand counterparts during their consultations. At other levels productive work developed with the Defence Department's Gordon Blakers, whom I considered to be one of the wisest and most experienced contributors to strategic thinking. Day-to-day cooperation outside the more stifling committee procedures accelerated when the Defence Group moved up to Canberra. Other Defence officials who contributed to memory and continuity were Gordon Poyser and Don Clues. Service officers working in these areas had less continuity because of the Service necessity of rotating officers. A more stable appointment at senior level was that of Rear-Admiral Alan McNicoll (later Sir Alan when he was appointed Chief of Naval Staff). External Affairs staffing in this area also needed to be improved. I had the customary Public Service problem of what to do with officers who did not measure up.

The grip of the past in the strategic outlook

There were misunderstandings on both sides. The ideas embedded in Service tradition grew out of the history of imperial defence, and subordinate attachment to allied commands wherever governments sent them. Much of our national history was so made.

During the 1950s Australia's defence concerns became more focused geographically. Leadership of the alliance fell on the Americans in the Pacific and the British in Malaya/Singapore. Our alliance did not specify a role for Australia, as the North Atlantic Treaty Organization did for its members. Casey, while Minister for External Affairs, tried without success to get access to American plans in the Pacific in order to see where Australia fitted. The Americans fended us off with the argument that they maintained flexible capabilities not tied to specific scenarios—and probably because our capabilities in respect of the Soviet Union and China were so limited that we should confine ourselves simply to maintaining operational compatibility with the Americans against the day when we might be needed somewhere in concert with them.

Not surprisingly therefore, the Services, in Defence Committee discussions, derived Australia's role from generalisations, such as 'limited war' of no defined location and 'support of allies'. In those days I saw no reason to object. The government of the day, while prudently avoiding commitment to some American ideas on new military engagements in the Pacific, subscribed to the view that our main defence lay in America honouring an obligation under the ANZUS Treaty. In party politics, the Menzies-led Coalition claimed a unique ability to ensure that support. Questioning whether there was certainty of that support, including military action in every circumstance, was forbidden as, to use the political jargon, 'downgrading ANZUS'.

In 1959 I argued in the Defence Committee for a strategic posture that called for more capabilities that could operate independently, from which Australian contributions to allied-led operations could be drawn. The idea was incorporated in the Strategic Basis recommendation sent up for Cabinet policy direction. It was rejected by Cabinet. I was later told by Sir Garfield Barwick that a senior Minister warned Cabinet that the concept was an invitation to the Chiefs to demand more money.[9] So much for national self-reliance.

I wanted to get competent officers into positions requiring dealings with the Defence Department and with British, American and other officials, in Canberra or in the respective capitals. Notable contributors from External Affairs were John Quinn (later an Ambassador tragically killed in an aircraft crash in North Africa), David (later Sir David) Hay, Alan Eastman, Robert Furlonger, and Malcolm Booker. Later others followed.

The substance of advice given to Ministers during these years is not part of this narrative. I am describing the awakening of my knowledge of defence matters on a road that was later to lead to a decade in the Defence Department. In these years I saw evidence of the high regard in which Australian Service officers were held by other countries for their standards of operational efficiency. I also began to form opinions that I retained in later years about their limitations in strategic analysis and about the grip on them of historical experience that was not always relevant to the present and the future. Inescapably I formed judgements about such matters as educational background and intellectual quality.

While External Affairs was much involved in these strategic assessments in the 1950s, we had no role in decisions about the shape of our defence capabilities. In earlier years Menzies had proclaimed 'we cannot stand alone'. In November 1959 the Defence Minister, Athol Townley, told Parliament that 'the primary aim of our defence effort should therefore be the continual improvement of our ability to react promptly and effectively with our allies to meet limited war situations'. There was ambiguity in the definition of 'threat' in Defence usage. Reflecting our historical engagement in allied operations worldwide, the term had an open-ended connotation, although the assumed area of any Australian military action was now much narrower.

By the early 1960s, Defence programming was putting more emphasis on a capacity to act independently. In 1963 Townley spoke of the desirability of being able to 'react ... by ourselves'. A trend in attitude was beginning to appear. Although the size of our forces increased little, it coincided with growing apprehension about developments to our immediate north, where the reactions of the Americans could not be predicted. The growing bellicosity of Sukarno, and the use of intimidation and some force to disrupt the incorporation of Borneo and Sabah into Malaysia, were frequently reviewed in the Defence Committee, which recommended increased defence provisions because of our long military association with Malaya. In these years it was a Defence axiom that threats could arise with little or no warning, demanding that adequate Australian forces be available for deployment.

America's definition of the ANZUS obligation

During 1963 Ministers became exercised over the uncertainties of US support should Australia have to protect Australian New Guinea and if military conflict with Indonesia were to arise from our commitment to come to the assistance of Malaysia. In February 1964 I was sent to Washington for discussions on these matters. During the course of the talks the Secretary of State, Dean Rusk, asked me pointedly whether Australia intended to increase its defence capabilities. I do not think that my subsequent report had any significant effect. Ministers were committed to promoting economic development projects (like so-called 'beef roads' in Queensland) under the constraints of an anti-inflation policy.

The Americans had longstanding reservations, rooted in their history, about defending British colonial interests in Southeast Asia. The consultations with the Americans brought home to the Australian Government that any US support to Australia with combat troops was neither guaranteed in advance nor unconditional. But this was the last thing for the Government to admit publicly. As to the adequacy of Australia's ability to deal with any Indonesian attack, Rusk said plainly to Hasluck in 1964 that the United States would expect to see conscription in any country supporting Malaysia before considering giving help themselves. I was impressed by the careful deliberation of his words as I heard them. Later, in November 1964, Cabinet approved the introduction of national service and increased provisions for defence. And the Prime Minister and Hasluck issued a decree that any further questioning of the Americans about their view of their ANZUS obligation must cease—presumably not wanting to risk an unpalatable public answer.

I had opportunities to meet the British commanders of all three Services, and I talked with the First Lord of the Admiralty, Peter (Lord) Carrington. I was with the Minister for External Affairs, Sir Garfield Barwick, when he met the US Navy team and the Justice Department officials to negotiate the terms of Australian consent to establishing their naval communications station at North West Cape. Apart from hearing Barwick rejecting many of their requests for privileged treatment with a lecture on the Federal Constitution, it was a useful introduction to the US Navy's global view, and the nuisance they found in other people's sovereignty.

I had a non-speaking part in various Prime Ministerial meetings with high-level visitors. There were ANZUS meetings, Southeast Asia Treaty Organisation meetings, and Commonwealth Ministerial meetings, and at all of them, in the 1950s and early 1960s, international security problems were part or the whole of the agenda.

These were years in which I sought help from the Services in improving my understanding of Service activities. The Chief of the Air Staff, Air Marshal Sir Valston Hancock, offered to show me, in a Canberra bomber aircraft piloted by himself, how a low-level attack could evade radar detection. I was disconcerted when his deputy, Colin Hannah, bluntly questioned my sanity and recommended I ask to be flown by a young flight lieutenant. Nevertheless the lesson from Hancock proceeded. The chosen day had intensely high temperatures and correspondingly high low-level turbulence. I had a trickle of blood from a stud in the canopy over the jump seat after we came in low over a beach east of Canberra and the Air Marshal, having lost radio contact, found that his appeals for permission to ascend to calm air were unheard and fruitless. He told me of his fear of structural damage until we bounced northward towards Richmond with radio restored. We landed for a needed respite before flying back to Canberra, our intended destination.

The year 1964 and early months of 1965 were my last as Secretary of External Affairs. They had a similarity with 1954 when I began. Our diplomacy continued to be dominated by concern in the Menzies Government for the country's security. Situations in Vietnam, Malaysia, and Indonesia were straining relations with allies. After a long period of nursing our relations with Indonesia with an eye to the longer term, we in External Affairs (criticised as we only later learned for being too conciliatory)[10] accepted that a military response might be necessary to curb Sukarno, while we could still hope for internal restraints on him. Measures to support the disintegrating government in South Vietnam were not my first priority because I could see no initiatives that Australia could effectively take. My newly appointed Minister (Hasluck) thought otherwise. In public statements by him and by the Prime Minister, the situation was seen as a downward thrust from China through satellites into Southeast Asia.

My own influence on policy in these matters was diminished. Symptomatic was the presentation to Cabinet of a Chiefs of Staff estimate (questionable in my opinion) on the possibility of holding a military line in South Vietnam, without the paper being accompanied by the customary External Affairs estimate of the likelihood of effective government with popular support. Hasluck would not have felt the need to have the Department advise him on such a matter.[11]

Earlier, in 1962, one of Barwick's first actions after succeeding Menzies as Minister for External Affairs was to address the Dutch–Indonesian dispute over the status of West New Guinea, and the inertia of Australian policy. He had taken some steps (which Menzies considered electorally risky for a Government with a majority of one) to persuade the public of the enduring need for good relations with our close neighbour. In the background was the certainty that the Dutch would not remain in the territory, and the public needed to be prepared. In 1961 I had myself warned Menzies in writing that the Dutch were certain to leave, and said his Government needed to decide what it would prefer to see in their place. When Barwick told Cabinet of the need for a process to settle the dispute, he was told not to take any initiative.

During 1963 Barwick told me that the Prime Minister had suggested the need to consider a change in the occupancy of the Secretary's post. Barwick implied that there was no hurry, but wanted suggestions as to where I would like to go. I had the impression that he would have liked me to stay on. It was only years later that I learned of the strength of Menzies' dissatisfaction with me and his determination to have me out (and that I was not to be offered the vacant Washington Embassy posting). As a result of this, Barwick asked again later for my decision. I expressed a preference for New Delhi, India, enabling an exchange to be made with Plimsoll if they accepted my recommendation that he succeed me in Canberra. Barwick then retired, but Hasluck, his successor, moved promptly to bring about the changes.

I remain uncertain of the reason for Menzies' displeasure, which he never expressed to me. Over the years my assessment of Australia's best interests in respect of nationalist struggles against colonialism, and the antipathy of some Asian leaders to Australia's military alignments, had sometimes differed markedly from his view when he encountered these issues in the Commonwealth and read reports of their treatment in the United Nations. Perhaps it was a matter of personality. There was some solace in the fact that, as will appear later in this narrative, four later Prime Ministers (Gorton, McMahon, Whitlam and Fraser) did not share Menzies' judgement. Each offered me appointments or responsibilities as Departmental Secretary or Ambassador in a major embassy.

Moreover, after some months of Hasluck's aloofness from his Department, his disapproval of being offered advice on policy, and his schoolmasterish scolding of senior officers on trivia of administration, I was personally pleased to be heading for New Delhi.

Interlude in India

New Delhi was not a professionally demanding post. Bilateral relations were cordial but constrained both politically and commercially. Relations had long been affected by the contrast between India's leadership of the Non-Aligned Movement (which was in fact weighted against the United States) and Australia's military alliance with the United States. Nothing that Australia said was likely to move India away from its opposition to the military intervention in support of South Vietnam, nor its calculated playing off of the United States against the Soviet Union while accepting American aid and being conciliatory to Moscow. Pressure from powers greater than Australia to negotiate with Pakistan over Kashmir would have been ineffective. The morass of bureaucratic regulation of the economy under an old-fashioned socialism frustrated Australian business investment.

Our substantial gifts of wheat during the food crisis earned us some goodwill in the Indian Government. I directed much of my energy to cultivating a better opinion of Australia in the influential print media and among members of the Lok Sabha (the lower House of Parliament). I doubt that I made much impression on the coterie preserving the Jawaharlal Nehru tradition (including his daughter Indira) and certainly not on the Defence Minister Krishna Menon, passionate defender of the Nehru faith. I recall that before I addressed a meeting of a young lawyers' association, he introduced me with a warning to my listeners that I was aligned with the United States. Such absurdities were not universal and I was on good terms with some younger Ministers who were prepared to listen. There were plentiful opportunities for speaking engagements around the country where English was in common use among those influencing policy and opinions.

I gave special attention to the role of the armed Services at a time of spreading separatist movements, as well as the unresolved border dispute with China, and the feud with Pakistan. Some observers were speculating about the possibility of an Army takeover, which I discounted. On the face of it, the Army had great power and undoubted popular prestige. I had several talks with the General (later Field Marshal) commanding Eastern Command whose force of 300 000 illustrated the point. The British tradition of keeping out of politics seemed secure. Candour with me was encouraged by respect for Australia's Service traditions and record, and for our historical British connection. I lectured often at senior Service establishments. There was limited sympathy there for the Soviet Union about which our intelligence assessors in Canberra showed interest, not least when the Indian Navy began to acquire Soviet submarines.

I learned more about British mess decorum in India than I did elsewhere. In speech and drill the customs of Sandhurst flourished, and their polo was certainly better. Nor was the Indian Navy an exception to the British tradition, judging by a scene on the grassy uplands of the Nilgiri Hills in the south as I approached the Wellington Staff College for one of my regular speaking engagements. A dishevelled rider in a red hunting jacket, tossed off his horse, was identified as a bearded Sikh naval captain. I learned that his quarry was a jackal because of the paucity of foxes.

Access to Bhutan was very restricted and only a handful of ambassadors were permitted entry. The Indian Army had at least one division deployed to protect the country's frontier with China. Its Chief (General Kumaramangalam) made arrangements direct with the King for him to receive me. A young Australian house-guest was greatly impressed to hear him say: 'I shall ring the King'.[12] The Air Force was more reclusive, perhaps because of heavy reliance on Soviet deliveries of equipment, and I found congenial relations to be more difficult. In contrast, an Army General, Sen, when in office had said, after dinner in the Australian High Commissioner's Residence, that he was leading a study of ways of conducting a successful coup against the Government. After a suitably dramatic pause he added that it was done at the request of the Minister for Defence, and had concluded that if any dissident command in the Hindu north were to start such a move, it would be quickly suppressed by loyal units from elsewhere.

There was time in India to reflect on the strategic assessments of my own country and the level of our defence preparation, while the Government dwelt on fears for national security. There was still a propensity, after Sukarno had been dislodged, to give more emphasis in Australia to our dependence on the ANZUS Treaty than to a sober estimate of Australia's own capability to look after itself. There was not much in India's policies to emulate. Yet, wrong-headed and hypocritical as India's policies sometimes were, one's mind was gripped by the undeviating direction of India towards national self-interest without concession to sentiment towards others, or to the 'loyalty' so evident in Australian official policies towards our 'traditional friends'.

I visited Vietnam twice during my New Delhi assignment, the better to understand the prospects of the Saigon Government. In 1967 the Australian Ambassador, L.H. Border, escorted me to three of the Corps Headquarters to meet local commanders and officials. I flew by helicopter to the Australian Task Force Headquarters at Nui Dat for a briefing from those in the field. In 1969 I visited Saigon again. On each occasion I was briefed by the American senior commander and given what a sceptical Australian Army officer described to me as the optimistic briefing customarily given to American Congressmen. I was also briefed by each of the Australian two-star generals serving at the so-called 'Free World' Headquarters. I was later to serve with each in Canberra.

In pursuing these interests as an External Affairs official, and reporting what I thought of the state of the South Vietnam's Government and my impressions of the US effort, I was influenced by my own conviction of the need for Australia to have a system to marry defence and foreign policy activities so as to produce sound security policy.

After India: Where to move?

By 1969 I was entering my fifth year and the fifth summer in India. The number of summers endured has been the traditional Western European's measure of a family's ability to survive the debilitating heat and the intestinal torments of the north Indian plain, particularly for anyone determined to get out of the air-conditioning and secure hygiene in order to meet Indians in their own environment throughout the country, as I did.

My time was coming to an end as 1970 approached. Before relating some twists and turns that finally were to place me in the Department of Defence, I should describe some correspondence in 1968, two years earlier, which might well have had an effect. I had then offered some gratuitous advice to an old friend, Sir Henry Bland, when I learned that he had been appointed Secretary of the Department of Defence in succession to Sir Edwin Hicks. Drawing on my accumulated judgement of the weaknesses in that Department in my dealings with it for over a decade, I wrote to Bland urging him to reform the system, and went on to argue why that was necessary:

> You may be asking what it has to do with me. Put it down to the exuberance of an early retirement and to eleven and a half years of participation in the Defence Committee. In fact I first attended Fred Shedden's performing animal show in Melbourne as an acting 'invited member' in about 1952. Chiefs of Staff have come and gone like a mirage

in a desert. But one visible and rocklike feature that remained with us always was the indomitable resistance of the Department of Defence to being itself the innovator of anything, or the original source of ideas on strategy, or choice of weapons, or defence associations with the outside world—or anything else. Accountancy and minute-taking have been its forte—from Secretary down. It has been heartbreaking—and sometimes frightening through the years. Time and again it has been EA [External Affairs] (whether its views were right or wrong) which has had to say—'Look! This is a problem. It needs an answer—by next Thursday. Please forget about the holiday weekend'. It has been partly mental sterility. But it has been more a deplorably wrong approach and system of administering the formulations of the 'defence view' of current international or domestic situations to say nothing of the determination of purely 'defence' questions like the choice of weapons systems—in respect of which I have no more knowledge than an outside listener but got an impression of the superficiality of much of the analysis.

So I hope you are going to import some brains and—more important—stimulate them and those that the Department already possesses, to come up with ideas without waiting for the Joint Service machinery or EA to speak first.

Which leads to the tripartite Joint Service machinery—with its Defence Department appendages, and EA participation where the subject matter is relevant. I do not believe that past methods of working the system are adequate for the needs of the past decade (much less the future). There is absolutely no stimulus to fresh thinking or re-analysis of traditional conclusions because Services inescapably argue from individual Service briefs and get no marks for supporting an innovation of ideas from another which might have ill consequences for their own. They are not stupid men. It is the system that is wrong. And, to compound the problem, the prime attitude of the Defence Department is, it seems, to remind all concerned of the past decisions on the question and to ensure that the commencement of the paper quotes the past decision. It is like starting a romance with your late wife's photograph in plain view—dampening to all. Tattered old clichés in papers coming up to the Defence Committee get sanctified as holy writ but the system abhors change.

A more balanced view than this of Bland's Department would acknowledge that some blame lay with the Coalition Governments for preserving four other Departments (Navy, Army, Air and Supply) over which the Defence Department had only partial control; and that the Defence Department's own methods had served the country well enough in the Second World War. My exaggerated language was aimed at moving Bland (himself an innovative reformer).

Moreover, when writing as I did, I had no thought of leaving External Affairs. I looked forward to further years in India and to the eventual possibility of heading one of the three major high commissions or embassies, although aware that two of them had been filled invariably by politicians.[13]

In March 1969 I was dismayed to be offered, by an inexperienced Minister for External Affairs (Gordon Freeth), a new position of Deputy High Commissioner in London to be created for me. I recalled the persistent unwillingness of High Commissioners there to allow any subordinate to have access to British Cabinet Ministers. In particular, the Australian High Commissioner in London from 1951 to 1956, Sir Thomas White (not the most discerning of intellectuals), had fended off an attempt by Menzies to have him bring External Affairs people in Australia House into high-level contacts. I rejected the idea of being inadvertently demoted in this way to talking only with officials. I asked for an ambassadorial position of responsibility such as Washington or Tokyo or London (in that order of preference), and otherwise to remain in India.

In Canberra five months later, dining with Freeth and later having Sunday morning drinks with John Gorton at the Lodge, I was offered the posting to Washington. Keith Waller (the incumbent) and I corresponded thereafter about arrangements for the takeover, preserving confidentiality as protocol required. I also wrote a critical commentary to my old friend Plimsoll on the loss of initiative in the Department of External Affairs and on the exclusion of officers from policy discussion with Ministers. On the basis of discussion with several officers, I attributed this in part to an inheritance from the stifling attitude of the former Minister, Paul Hasluck. This had a sequel.

The Defence Department appointment

Administration under Gorton was often unorthodox, sometimes scornful of convention and prevailing lines of authority, and affected by the Prime Minister's preferences for particular individuals. These habits extended to his relations with some of his Cabinet colleagues, as I was to observe more than once at close quarters. Early on 21 November 1969, as I was dressing for the day, the Residence Head Bearer/Major Domo (Shafiq Mohammed Ali) ascended the stairs in an excited state crying: 'Sahib! Sahib! There is a man on telephone from Australia wanting to speak to Sahib and I am telling him it is not right time and please go away, but he is angry man. I am not knowing his name because telephone is not good—something like "Gorton".' After expressing hasty apologies to the Prime Minister, I heard him say that he and the Defence Minister, Malcolm Fraser, wanted me to succeed Sir Henry Bland who had suddenly decided to retire because of his wife's indifferent health. Having said I would do whatever he thought best, I made a point of saying that I had no experience as a member of any of the Services. He said this did not matter. I suggested that Fraser discuss the timing with my newly appointed Minister, William McMahon.

Four days later McMahon rang me to say that he would like me to return as Secretary of the Department of External Affairs (re-named Foreign Affairs in 1970), as he thought it best if Plimsoll moved on. I told him I thought that much needed attention in the Department as a result of Plimsoll's administrative shortcomings, but this was not for me as I was now committed elsewhere. McMahon said he had been kept in the dark by Gorton and Fraser over the Defence appointment offer and would consult his colleagues. Asked which Department I preferred, I said External Affairs. (On reflection later I decided that my return would not have been good for the Department.) In another telephone call to New Delhi, McMahon said that the Prime Minister had only then confirmed what had been going on in the dark. In a cable, through commercial channels, he asked me to report on the Department's deficiencies that I had referred to, and to give him an assessment of the officers whom I thought ought to be considered to replace Plimsoll. I wrote doing so, in my own hand without keeping any copy, recommending Waller. Waller was in fact appointed. Lest my view of Plimsoll should be misinterpreted, I should add that in overseas missions—and he headed all of our major ones as no other career officer had done—Plimsoll was unique in his ability, perhaps our best. People at the top, including difficult people like Syngman Rhee in Korea, opened their doors to him. Administration of a large Department and nurturing its staff were, however, not his forte.

The announcement was made and I made my farewells in India. On the way back to Australia I made some visits to gather information that would be more difficult to make in my new capacity without media speculation—Tokyo, the American supply base on Okinawa, and Jakarta.

> You will get on much better than our Defence Secretary because you know nothing about weapons whereas he has been there too long and thinks he knows a lot.

An Indian Chief of the Naval Staff said this to me as I departed for Canberra in January 1970. Would the same be said about me nine years hence?

Defence Minister Fraser: His strategic outlook

The leisurely pace of the Department under Edwin Hicks that I visited during the 1960s had changed. Bland had started many changes. Fraser, who was 39, had been in office only a matter of weeks and already the staff were experiencing his demands with urgent timetables attached. He intended to make a far-reaching statement on defence policy, to bring to decision outstanding matters (not least the delivery of the problem-plagued F-111 aircraft which had the Government under continuous attack from the Opposition and the media), and to record his view of Australia's strategic priorities. Bland for his part was trying to round up quickly, before departure, the many enquiries, proposed reforms in inter-Service collaboration, and central staffing reorganisation that he had initiated under Allen Fairhall.

Fraser made his statement on 10 March 1970.[14] He recapitulated and endorsed the reforms that his predecessor (Fairhall) had approved on Bland's advice. On strategy he promised ambitious policies: to reject isolation; to involve Australia in the processes of change in Southeast Asia and the surrounding Pacific Ocean and Indian Ocean waters; to prepare Australian forces for regional security; to maintain the focus on Malaya and Singapore; to make our forces more self contained; and to include an offensive capacity.

In later years, after experiencing the failure of successive governments to finance a capability which lived up to these ambitions, I began to recognise the Fraser statement to be in this respect at one with those of the Menzies Government earlier: to make commitments for sound diplomatic reasons which outran the Government's later willingness to provide the defence capabilities to implement them. Eventually Australia had to narrow its focus away from the wider visions of Spender, Casey and their successors, and to concentrate more on capabilities to defend our own soil and nearer neighbourhood, abandoning some strategic capabilities for more distant operations for which finance could not be found.

Some years had to pass before advocates of a comprehensively equipped Defence Force were forced to accept choices and priorities among Fraser's objectives. It was to prove a long drawn-out effort to bring the Services to accept the unpalatable. And it took longer—long after my time—before Ministers accepted narrower strategic objectives and the need to bring defence capabilities into line with those more limited strategic interests, under a limited budget and accepting traditional popular opposition to compulsory Army service. In this process, rejection of capabilities is fiercely fought by the interested Service and its parliamentary supporters, is disliked by allies, and requires courage by Ministers. The eventual abandonment of Australia's aircraft carrier with its distant blue-water capabilities is an example.

A common outlook had to be achieved. Fraser made a prescient remark, only months after President Richard Nixon's 1969 forecast at Guam of reduced American world policing: 'We need to ensure that each of the Services prepares for the same kind of conflicts, in the same places, and in the same time scale.'

An encouraging aspect of Fraser's speech was the fact that he surveyed the world situation and gave strategic objectives—over-ambitious or not—their status as the foundation of defence activities (incidentally earning a rebuke from McMahon for intrusion into his Foreign Affairs territory). Previous statements and public comment tended to focus endlessly on the adequacy (or inadequacy) of ships, aircraft, weapons and Army manpower, without focus on where Australian interests were likely to require these military assets to be actually used. Geographic focus was missing and was usually submerged in the concept of ensuring 'balance' and 'operational compatibility with allies'. As I shall suggest later, there was powerful resistance that grew out of our historical national allegiances which were the basis of traditions within the Services themselves, before a Minister for Defence was able to say with an authority not previously existing: 'The Defence policy of the Government is to pursue a disciplined relationship between strategy and force structure within the constraints of what is financially feasible'.[15]

New to the scene in January 1970, I made no significant contribution to the Fraser statement. My first priorities were to take hold of a large system, to learn about it, and to consolidate the Bland reforms.

The Fairhall/Bland Reforms inherited

During 16 years in the industrial relations world as Secretary of the Department of Labour and National Service, Bland had demonstrated confidence in his own opinions and readiness to enter a fight undaunted by rank or odds. These were qualities eminently suitable for one about to enlarge Ministerial control and impose unified objectives on the Services' expenditure and activities.

By mid-1968 Bland had persuaded his Minister, Allen Fairhall, to agree to innovations to achieve these results. One method was to cease to rely in the Department on the committees to which each Service sent its representative, unavoidably connected with satisfying the interest of the Service; and to replace them with officers, chosen for their qualities, to serve for some years in the Department as members of a joint staff in an environment conducive to more objective analysis. Another innovation called for a system of analysing proposals that each Service made for a place in the Defence Minister's expenditure programme for ships, aircraft and their weapons systems (and, in the case of the Army particularly, for manning levels). This would involve the Joint Staff. In what turned out in subsequent years to be one of the most controversial aspects of the reform, Fairhall decided that qualified civilians were to join in the process. Bland set about recruiting such civilians.

The second leg of the reforms was to create a methodical system of keeping under regular review commitments to future expenditure, tabulated according to the year of impact on the budget, and to keep such commitments within an annual limit laid down by Ministers. They made no commitment to the figures, which were known only as 'financial guidance'. Proposed commitments would be judged by the analysis process for their conformity to the official strategic outlook, subordinating single-Service ambitions to collective defence priorities.

Bland sent officers to study the Rand Corporation system used by the US Secretary of Defense, Robert McNamara. It was later adopted as the Five Year Defence Rolling Program—'rolling' because there was an annual review of outlays forecast and adjustments made to the content where necessary, whether because of changes in cost, or of delivery or other problems. I believe Gordon Blakers gave Bland the idea after Blakers had had a briefing by the Pentagon on the Rand concept of applying the test of cost-effectiveness to proposals to acquire new weapons and other capabilities. It rested on detailed questioning of their conformity to endorsed strategy, to priorities in the approved programme, and to financial limits. The so-called Planning, Programming and Budgeting System demanded disciplined analysis. The Defence Department was the first to introduce this forward programming into Canberra administration in the face of Treasury scepticism. It was many years before the system was widely adopted elsewhere in Commonwealth Departments.

Fraser adopted the new system, but its introduction required new procedures and there was latent resistance to change. The desire remained to safeguard the power of decision by professional Service officers in the interests of their Service, and perhaps of members of the specialised branches for which they had been trained and where their careers lay. In their view, the Defence Department did not understand Service needs and was a predominantly civilian Department, not all of whose staff was of the high quality that should accompany the power of saying 'no'. Possibly some high-handedness contributed to a mood of non-cooperation.

Understandably Bland, in his 24 months, had been unable to reform entrenched Service attitudes towards each other and towards the Department of Defence and its Minister. I came to believe that nothing less than a kind of cultural change over time had to be the objective. Tribalism is not eliminated solely by making new rules. Progress was made in my time. But it took decades, a succession of Labor Governments committed to reform, and the arrival of a new generation of more liberally educated Service officers, before it could be said that there was no turning back from the reforms that had their genesis in 1968.

After Bland retired for family reasons, he was justifiably commended in editorials of major journals. He later expanded his views on defence reorganisation in the 1970 Roy Milne Memorial Lecture, following Lieutenant General Sir Leslie Morshead's idea of fewer Departments.[16] When I later developed my own views on that matter, I did not adopt Bland's particular solution.

The scope of the Defence Group empire

In the year that I came to the Defence Department, the Defence Group's 1970–71 budget was responsible for 14 per cent of total Commonwealth expenditure, and was estimated to be 3.6 per cent of the Gross National Product. Much of this was attributed to our operational expenditure in respect of Vietnam. As I was later to discover, other requirements were neglected. The number of civilian staff, mostly dedicated to activities in the Service commands, was very large. The Defence Group's activities were widely dispersed geographically. They required the services of a wide range of professional personnel in shipbuilding; aircraft and arms and stores production; scientific research and its application to the repair and the modification of equipment to unique Australian climatic and other conditions; health services; and much more. There were establishments for education, and others for training in the advanced technologies employed in weapon controls and the sensors needed for all environments. The range of activities sustained by the Defence vote was a microcosm of Commonwealth Government administration across the board, as well as of much within the province of State administrations. Relations with allies had to be fostered and disagreement negotiated away. Important intelligence-gathering systems and analyses of the product had to be managed.

I had to remedy my lack of knowledge of the way each Service managed itself, and of the operational requirements that lay behind each Service's submissions to Defence for financial approvals. In the equipment area each Service had its own philosophies, based on accumulated experience in combat, on such matters as survivability in conflict, life in service, acceptable rate of obsolescence, and maintainability under Australian conditions. Those conditions included the physical environment (such as the hot wet and hot dry climate), paucity of ports, distance from bases, as well as the country's industrial capability to meet requirements or to modify equipment without dependence on distant countries of origin.

Five Defence Group Ministries: Previous unsuccessful reforms

It soon became apparent to me that I had to clarify the authority I derived from the Minister. Fundamental to this was to get recognition of his authority over the constituent parts of the Defence Group, particularly the Army, the Air Force and the Navy. The Department of Supply, while jealous of its autonomy, was under Public Service management and more amenable to guidance.

Fairhall had in writing called on the Defence Group Ministers to cooperate with the system instituted by him on Bland's advice. But before the end of 1970, I could see some of the problems that Fraser had in consulting and winning the cooperation of these Ministers. They were based far apart, while Fraser made his home in Canberra. Each had full Ministerial status, yet none (apart from the Minister for Supply) was a member of the Cabinet where financial and foreign policy restraints were debated and policy decided. The Service Ministers were not privy to the documentation and high-level assessments in which their own Chiefs of Staff shared. Nevertheless, each Service expected its Minister to give parliamentary and public support, to foster morale and to acknowledge the Service's achievements.

In 1970 the total number of regulars in the three Services was 84 000. The system of control had long been an anachronism. It had been designed for management of more than a million Navy, Army and Air Force personnel during the Second World War, serving commands remote from each other around the world under various higher commands (usually allied). When they were brought together back in Australia to satisfy peacetime priorities with drastically reduced numbers, there was rivalry between Services pursuing different strategic concepts with not always consistent military capabilities. It is reasonable to speculate that the rivalry was made more likely by the weakness in the system of Ministerial oversight. Fraser, not a notably patient man, found that consultation with the Service Ministers—James Killen (Navy), Andrew Peacock (Army) and Senator Tom Drake-Brockman (Air)—was impeded by their being scattered around Australia from North Queensland to the Northwest of Western Australia, while Fraser resided and worked in Canberra. They complained, and he complained.

What should have been fundamental to the authority of the Defence Minister was the Menzies 'directive' of 1958. At that time, the Prime Minister had explained to Parliament his Cabinet's rejection of the Morshead Committee's recommendation that it abolish the Service Departments and the decision to adopt the alternative of issuing a firm declaration giving the Defence Minister overall policy command. When I came into the Department 12 years later, I did not find anyone who knew of the directive; nor did the Service leaders acknowledge its significance. In formal papers leading to decisions or to recommendations to the Government, the Menzies directive was never quoted.

The Menzies solution to the disunity and lack of adequate central control in the Defence system was, in my view, a failure. It may be that a lethargic Defence Department in the late 1950s and early 1960s was at fault in not vigorously keeping before the top layer of the Services, always moving between Canberra and their commands, their responsibility to observe the directive. Or there may have been a convenient amnesia. In any case, there was probably a deeper cause of resistance to supervision by the Defence Minister of the professional activities of the Service Chiefs. They enjoyed—or claimed—the right to go over the head of their Minister to the Prime Minister. I occasionally heard officers flirting with the idea that the Governor-General's constitutional status as commander-in-chief had practical application, although I did not hear this disturbing view of responsible government from any of the Chiefs of Staff.

Respect for the authority of the civil power was never in question. They were entitled to say (and often did) that civil servants were not the civil power. At the same time, I believe that public servants did find in the Services differences from their own instinctive respect for Ministerial authority, and from their desire to assist Ministers to the utmost, whether asked or not. Service leaders are understandably conscious of the unique nature of their profession, requiring as it does dedication to a duty to put their lives at risk in a way not shared by any other. I would expect that keeping Ministers out of trouble politically would not be much on their mind.

To reform practices within the military command system required military, not civilian, leadership. The Menzies decision had created the office of Chairman of the Chiefs of Staff Committee, placed in the Department and answering direct to the Minister, with a rank higher than that of the Chiefs. When I entered the Department, the Chairman was General Sir John Wilton, then approaching the end of a four-and-a-half year term. Bland had told me of some differences between them. Wilton was a friend of mine from my External Affairs days and we had that advantage in managing our relationship. But he was a taciturn man and I found this inhibiting when discussing with him ideas about reforms. Wilton was chafing under his lack of power of command over the Services and his somewhat obsessive interest in this remedy for deficiencies in policy directions of the Defence Group. While as a civilian I expected that, given goodwill, persuasion could be exercised by the Chairman of the Chiefs of Staff Committee, I was aware that command had to be legally based because of implications for life and death. The more relaxed and informal attitudes in the Public Service were not wholly applicable and would not survive endemic rivalries over resources and power. In later discussions of the reforms under Labor, I learned how often a proposal for change might be judged by where the power of decisions would reside in a changed arrangement, rather than by the intrinsic merits of change.

Some writers have attributed intellectual qualities to Wilton that I did not discover.[17] He gave me (as he had done to Bland) his proposed changes in the chain of authority. I was unwilling to give his ideas priority over many other reforms that had been initiated and not brought to fruition, and others that were needed.

In any case I was wary of his objective, as Bland had been. This was justified when I became aware (from reading an essay by Ian McNeill)[18] of Wilton's memoirs. He had expressed his desire that submissions to the Minister, apparently irrespective of subject, be made by the military Chief rather than by the Departmental Secretary. Perhaps this debate had gone on in the Army Department earlier. To convert the Defence Department into a military command headquarters in this way (as might be found, for example, in Indonesia) was something no government was likely to tolerate. Menzies' Coalition Cabinet—the more likely of the two alternative parties to grant status to the Services—had specifically given, as a reason for its opposition to the abolition of the Service Ministers, that the consequential disappearance of the Public Service Departmental Secretaries would give too much authority to the Service Chiefs.

Managing the Department with limited powers

For me in 1970 there was much to learn about the requirements of each Service and what went on inside each of their different systems. Weapons procurement apart, Defence could only exert influence through its right of approval of total budget allocations and major weapons acquisitions. Attitudes did not help. The Defence Department was seen as an outsider—a primarily civilian regulatory Department, no more welcome to involve itself in Service decisions than was an analogous Department, the Treasury. The vast area of expenditures and decisions on maintenance and running costs, which imposed commitments on future budgets, remained a mystery to me. There was some confirmation that the secretaries of the Service Departments had their difficulties too, despite their responsibility under the law to safeguard economy in expenditure. In 1968 W.J. Curtis, then Deputy Secretary in Defence under Bland after long experience in the Army Department, spoke of that Department's lack of penetration into Army activity. Entry into this area by the Defence Department had to await the progressive introduction of the programming of intended expenditures, with a ceiling which provided an incentive to establish higher and lower priorities. In the absence of such a system, only resolute military leadership would have made any progress. Parliament had many former officer members ready to protect one Service or another against change, particularly if it involved unwelcome civilian initiatives.

For the new Departmental Secretary in the Fraser years, 1970 and 1971, there was more to defence administration and policy advice than battling over reforms to the antiquated system. There were intelligence arrangements with allies to deal with; defence arrangements with Singapore and Malaysia (whose relations with each other were deteriorating); the consequences of supporting our forces in Vietnam; and major weapons procurement. Meetings had to be attended in Singapore and Wellington. There were some problems in the Department following the influx of Service officers, and the Fairhall/Bland exhortation for them to take a 'Defence' rather than a single-Service approach to their duties. There were a few cases when exploratory ideas about reforms, still not considered at the policy level, were rushed off secretly to the Service that might be affected, leading to premature reactions and occasionally appeals to sympathetic journalists. This was no way to encourage people to put to paper innovative thinking about possible reforms. Civilians in the Department became wary. I was probably at fault for withholding access by these Service officers to departmental files. But, with time, a more trusting atmosphere developed, as all wrestled with the procedures for introducing defence programming for the ensuing five years.

My wish to get out of Canberra in 1970 in order to visit the commands and operational units was frustrated by having to attend to jurisdictional disputes of the kind described. I concluded that Bland had introduced too many rationalisation studies, and too many changes to the practices required of the Services, in too short a time. Moreover, to be successful, the changes required Service officers to look for solutions without bias towards their own Service. There was no less a requirement to find civilians who understood the needs and ethos of the Services, but also with the intellectual ability to be innovative, and the stuffing to stand up for what they believed. Such people were hard to find in sufficient numbers in the Defence Group. Many in the geographic commands, like the stereotypical 'Colonel's clerk', acquiesced in Service authority. Tempers were frayed by some Defence Department demands with short timetables, and by some ideas of doubtful utility put to the Services. Some emollient was needed, as well as new priorities for our activities.

I let some of Bland's inquiries run down. I gave high priority to the handful of officers (principally John Moten and John Enfield) who were drawing up the procedures for the new system of defence programming. Time had to be given to explaining the system to officers at all relevant levels, and to circumventing the sceptics about the McNamara method of control.

Its significance for the authority of the Defence Minister and his advisers went much further. With the exception of large capital expenditure items, which would go to Cabinet individually, Treasury would cease to be concerned with the detail of expenditure of the Services and Supply. The Defence Department, consulting within the Defence Group, would become the system's treasury, acting within the overall expenditure limit agreed with Treasury.

There were weaknesses and anomalies. The rights of the Defence Group Ministers and of the Service Boards remained intact in legislation. Central scrutiny of the expenditure on the running costs of the Services and the group's factories and science laboratories, under their respective systems of authorisation, was impossible. As to decisions on equipment procurement, with the foreseeable related manning and maintenance expenditures they would generate, I concentrated on having this major aspect of the Secretary's financial responsibilities put to systems analysis by a mixed committee of qualified Public Service and uniformed officers. As I said earlier, this area of control in the Department was to become the focal point of controversy and objection to civilian intervention throughout my years in the Defence Department.

In his Defence Report published in September, Fraser said:

> The application of systematic analysis to the Services' proposals does not imply any intention to replace judgement by analysis. That is plainly impossible. On the other hand, the factors that have been referred to (the interest of local manufacturers), and the increasing military technology and its rapid rate of change, make it increasingly unlikely that reliance can be placed solely on unsupported judgement. Judgement must be complemented by the systematic analysis of alternative solutions—taking account of benefits and costs.

In effect, the intention was to displace the traditional Service 'requirement', with its mandatory connotation, with the more supplicant term 'bids'. Terminology is important. If Fraser realised what an uphill battle it would be, given the existing Ministerial arrangements, he did not admit it publicly for understandable reasons. The Opposition would have loved it.

Fraser's initiatives—and conflicts with Gorton

My early months working under Fraser were spent chiefly on establishing the new administrative apparatus already described, rather than on policy advising. Fraser for his part was still wrestling with the withdrawal of troops from Vietnam, in the atmosphere of public passion and protest that had built up over many months. I had not experienced this. In India, with no television and only meagre radio reports from Australia, my eyes had been on that country's turmoil, its military tensions and its conflicts with its neighbours. I was told of Fraser's earlier attempt, when he was Army Minister, to start an orderly withdrawal of ground troops from Vietnam. It had been difficult to calibrate such a withdrawal with unpredictable American withdrawals in a way that avoided appearing simply to do what the Americans did. I learned of Fraser's belief in using skills within Army units in forms of civil assistance to the community to foster support for the Saigon Government.

Handling our military presence in Vietnam, with its conscripted component, in the face of popular protests, was a major preoccupation for Fraser. But he had also committed himself, in his 10 March 1970 statement, to a programme of extensive changes. In addition, there was another burning problem—the Government's failure to achieve delivery of the F-111, the subject of accusations of mounting costs and Labor taunts in Parliament.

Fraser decided that the delivery problem had to be solved. There was a sharp difference with the Air Force over our insistence on bringing defence scientists in to advise him on the feasibility of the Americans solving the metal fatigue problem that had crippled the retractable wing system of the aircraft. The Air Force relied on its powerful engineering branch to monitor the situation. I had no doubt that it also wanted to preserve its exclusive relations with the US Air

Force, whose goodwill they might lose if our negotiating tactics impacted on the US Air Force budget.

Believing the long-running controversy in Parliament to be politically intolerable, Fraser led a team to Washington. He made me a member, along with the Secretary of the Air Department (Fred J. Green) and the Chief of Air Staff (Air Marshal Colin Hannah). On the eve of meeting the Americans, Fraser assembled his team for a late Sunday night session in the Australian Embassy chancery to try out various ways of approaching the Americans. Playing devil's advocate, Fraser shot down most of the arguments that we suggested, based on our agreement to accept supply of an airworthy F-111. Following loss of sleep during the journey to Washington, the occasion overwhelmed both Hannah and Green; one of them went to bed for several days.

Fraser doubted that the Air Department's conciliatory approach would give us satisfaction. He decided to go over the head of both Air Forces. He presented to Secretary of Defense, Melvin Laird, a largely political case about the damage to defence relations. He reminded the American that the Labor Opposition, who had attacked the transaction from the beginning, took a different view of our ANZUS association with the Americans. Fraser asked, in effect, that the Americans produce a viable aircraft or give us our money back. As Fraser himself has subsequently recorded,[19] the venue of the negotiation shifted from the Pentagon to a stadium holding a baseball game that Laird wanted to watch. Perched on uncomfortable benches among shouting spectators, in an atmosphere redolent of hot dogs, the two negotiators went on with their business.

After stressing the need for a viable aircraft in our joint strategic interests, Fraser accepted an offer to lease F-4 *Phantom* aircraft to bridge the gap until the F-111 problem was solved. Eventually we took delivery of this technologically advanced aircraft at a cost that was, in the context of rapidly rising prices, relatively modest, despite Opposition claims to the contrary.

Before returning to Australia, Fraser and I had a welcome diversion visiting mutual friends at their vacation retreat on the Virginia coast. William Battle, a wartime friend of John Kennedy, had been his Ambassador in Canberra during Fraser's early days in Parliament and mine in External Affairs.[20]

Back at home, Fraser decided to satisfy Service grievances over pay and conditions, a subject on which he felt I had been unduly cautious. Slowness of the legal authorities in drafting regulations to adjust pay (for example for the Navy's technicians) compounded the deficiencies of an earlier decision imposed on the Department and the Services. This had aligned their pay to civilian awards, a system that was incapable of recognising the command responsibilities of non-commissioned officers in the Services. This was creating anomalies and resentments as pay levels followed, after long delays, the wage blow-outs then prevalent in the civilian economy. A report by Justice Kerr defined for the first time a distinct profession of arms and a system of matching pay to responsibilities.

In this and other ways Treasury intrusion into Defence management had reduced the Department's standing in the eyes of Service personnel. Bland had only recently got the Treasury out of controlling the works programmes of the Services in their various bases and establishments. It took time to wear down Treasury's parsimony over the housing provided for other ranks.

Fraser called for a prompt study of the feasibility of locating a task force in Western Australia. He was disinclined to accept the Army's reservations and typically slow responses. I was more sympathetic to the Army's argument that it would be inefficient, and costly for training, to have to bring the task force together with specialists located on the east coast. I thought that Fraser's motivation was probably political, with an eye to the Western Australian electorate, which complained of its lack of defence protection. The idea died, but not before distrust of the Army developed.

I had my own frustrations with the Army and with the Army Department. There was an absence of candour or willingness to admit the existence of a problem that Defence could help to solve. Getting the right outcome for the totality of the defence effort required a shared belief in that objective rather than solutions sought by one Service in isolation from the others. I had to live with this insistence by all the Service Departments on their domestic jurisdiction, but it was the Army that was the most reluctant.

The Army was involved in one of Fraser's setbacks, but it was only one of several actions by the Prime Minister, Gorton, that gave it importance. The Prime Minister took it upon himself to authorise a call-out of the Pacific Islands Regiment, to provide a legal basis should the Administrator (Sir David Hay) later decide it was necessary to use troops to quell an uprising in New Guinea. In so acting, the Prime Minister overrode Fraser's earlier decision not to recommend the action to the Governor-General. My advice supported Fraser's view, as I believed there would be damage to the Army's image and that of Australia if Australian-led soldiers were used against indigenous people in a trust territory before civilian policing had demonstrably failed. The Governor-General (Sir Paul Hasluck, who had been a Territories Minister) asked whether the proposal had Cabinet backing. The matter did not come to a head as, in the event, the Administrator did not call out the Pacific Islands Regiment.

There were other setbacks. Gorton's reservations led Cabinet to postpone indefinitely the creation of a tri-Service academy recommended by a committee chaired by Sir Leslie Martin. (The title 'Australian Defence Force Academy' was only established some years later on my recommendation.)

I was not involved in yet another event involving Fraser and Gorton which developed into a crisis leading to the departure of both men from Ministerial office and which prepared the way for the downfall of the Coalition Government within two years. The situation arose out of Fraser's determination to exercise his authority over the way in which the Army command was acting in Vietnam, not in respect of its military operations in Phuoc Tuy province but in its dealings with the Saigon Government and others over civic assistance to local communities. His channel for conveying his questions and instructions was the newly appointed Chairman of the Chiefs of Staff Committee, Admiral Sir Victor Smith. I saw the Secretary as having no more than a watching role in respect of conformity to government policy by the Services in such operations, as I was not a proper channel for instructions where commands were needed.

After a visit to Vietnam to survey the political situation, the prospects of the Saigon Government, and the progress in pacification of the countryside, Fraser had come away dissatisfied with progress. He believed that reporting from Saigon through military and embassy channels was fragmented and inadequate. Taking a close interest in policy issues, he directed the Joint Intelligence Organisation, which served the inter-departmental National Intelligence Committee, to gather more information on the situation. The Director of the Joint Intelligence Organisation, Robert Furlonger, having no intelligence-gathering function, informed the Army of the task he had been given and sought their cooperation.

In February and early March 1971, a crisis of misunderstanding and distrust began, fuelled by unauthorised statements to the media in Saigon suggesting, wrongly, that Defence policy towards the continuation of 'civic action' had changed. It was further fuelled by an outrageously inaccurate report in the Sydney *Daily Telegraph* that the Joint Intelligence Organisation had been instructed to report on what the Army was doing, with the implication of spying on them.

There was substance in Fraser's indignant belief that the Army was acting on the assumption that, because the total withdrawal of the Army could be foreseen, forms of aid to the civil community (such as new building, medical assistance and so forth) should be reduced to those that could be completed before the withdrawal. As Fraser believed that some Army activity (such as that of the engineers) could continue after the remainder had withdrawn to Australia, he objected strongly to the Army's creating new policies and letting them appear in the media. Whether this was in fact the case, or just a suggestion in Army planning papers, is obscure. Fraser preferred to believe the former. He was, it seems, conducting his own unacknowledged briefing of selected media, making clear his disapproval of Army actions in Vietnam over civic action.

At this point the Prime Minister made another imprudent entry into Fraser's domain.[21] Having read (as he later explained publicly) media reports of actions by Fraser deleterious to the Army's reputation, he spoke, not to his Minister to satisfy his disquiet, but to the Chief of the General Staff (Lieutenant General Sir Thomas Daly) to obtain his view of events. What was said during the discussion is in contention. A prominent journalist wrote a story saying that Daly had complained of Fraser's disloyalty to the Army. Gorton left this statement unchallenged by not denying it.

Fraser reacted strongly. While not involved in this deteriorating situation, I had become aware, from discussions with Fraser over some months, of his critical view of the way Gorton conducted his office. When undermined in this way, he called me to his office to tell me of his decision to resign. I considered this to be a political matter and confined myself to advising on some of the formalities that Fraser would have to observe. Having set the process in motion, Fraser told me a day or two later that Gorton had offered some reconciliation. We discussed the steps already taken to give effect to the resignation. Fraser decided that he would go on with it. I took no part in his preparation of his resignation announcement in Parliament (privately I thought the language a little exaggerated). He was gracious and generous in saying farewell to officers of the Department.

Defence lost a strong and purposeful leader, better in these respects than any Coalition Minister for Defence up to the time of my retirement in 1979, and possibly better than any predecessor. His statement on 10 March 1970 of intended reforms, some of which he had inherited, was a remarkable survey of defects needing to be fixed. Whether he would have been strong enough to bring them about, had he remained in office, cannot be known. While always determined to get his own way, his insistence on consulting colleagues when Prime Minister later has been commended by some as desirable practice.[22] On my observation of him in Defence, I incline to the view that he needed the reassurance of support before acting. One needed reform he did not attempt was abolition of the Service Ministers. On that he would not have had the support of his Prime Minister, Gorton.

He had opinions about most things and was sometimes impetuous in forming them. He expected his advisers to disagree with him and some found his personality hard to endure. He was not always considerate enough to recognise the pressures felt by some. Setting short timetables for production of results by his subordinates maintained his reputation for vigour as a Minister, but it sometimes made for unreasonable demands on those serving him. Sunday night had to be accepted as a normal working time if it happened to suit him.

As to my own relations, Fraser told me in later years that, when considering names for Bland's successor, he rejected several names because, as he put it, 'I wanted someone who was willing to disagree with me'. It was not long before I had to oblige him. It was, as I recollect, over an administrative matter—his wanting one of my staff for an assignment when I said I needed him elsewhere. We exchanged one or two testy minutes before he brought the tiff to an end with an admirable solution: 'Before writing further formal notes I ask you to come over and discuss the matter that apparently disturbs you. It might be best to come at an hour when we can put a whisky in our hands.'

He had much to do with my decision to acquire a trout fishing haven in the mountains, blessed by the absence of a telephone or easy access. But there was never any rancour in our relations. Indeed, we shared a common love of fly-fishing. After becoming Prime Minister, he gave my wife and me the pleasure of having him as our guest at my haven.

Gorton the Defence Minister

Gorton had the portfolio for five months until McMahon dismissed him. Press verdicts on Gorton made much of his inability as a Minister to shake off the imperial style of Prime Ministership. I thought that in his relations with his new department he behaved very much the way Gorton always had—unorthodox, unconventional, not easy to persuade where his sense of loyalty to some group was involved, and prone to leaving his administrators in some uncertainty while he did what he had made up his mind to do. At the same time, one knew that Gorton had intellectual qualities of a kind seldom found among Defence Ministers.

He was confident of his own judgement on policy matters. While he did not tell his Department, as Hasluck had done in External Affairs, to speak on policy matters only when spoken to, he did not encourage policy advice. I had had an altercation with him years earlier when he was Minister Assisting the Minister for External Affairs. When he disputed, in brusque and uncompromising language, my right to vet expenditure proposals made to him by the Director of the Antarctic Division of the Department, I confronted him. The encounter ended in a draw. I am sure his respect for the adventurous Antarctic explorers was greater than his respect for chair-bound staff. Memory of this episode set me wondering how he would respond to the current programme of expanding the Defence Department's oversight of Service activities. The matter was not put to the test before he left the portfolio. I had no reason to foresee any personal distrust in as much as he had himself as Prime Minister offered me the Washington Embassy posting and later had personally asked me in that phone call to New Delhi to accept the diversion to the Defence Department sought by Fraser.

He showed his independence from his officers in ways unusual for a Minister. When Cabinet in mid-year called for a A$50 million cut in the Defence budget, he personally walked the rounds of the three Service buildings at Russell on a Sunday morning, trying out what cuts they could wear. Meanwhile his Departmental Secretary sat in his office waiting to be handed the scrap of paper recording Gorton's findings. A Chief of Staff later confided to me that he thought that Gorton had 'cooked the books' in his favour.

In a debate over the size of the Army, Gorton overrode the objective of both his Departmental Secretary and the Chairman of the Chiefs of Staff Committee to reduce Army manpower, in order to satisfy the requirement for better capabilities in other Services. The opposition he could expect from Army sympathisers might have given his Prime Minister the opportunity to 'get' him. Perhaps this was indeed in Gorton's mind. Gorton's rejection of a proposal, unanimously supported by the Service Chiefs, to place over the individual Service medical officers a superior medical officer answering to the Chairman of the Chiefs of Staff Committee was a bad omen for any new rationalisation efforts.

He showed his independence from previous Coalition attitudes in areas that I personally found encouraging. He had formed his own views on external defence relations while Prime Minister (and they appeared in an address to the Imperial Service Club in Sydney), for which he had not looked to the Department for advice.[23] He attacked some over-simplified slogans that had long been at the heart of the Coalition's policies in its conflict with the Labor Party over whether Australia's strategy needed forward bases and deployments. This was the conflict between 'forward defence' and 'fortress Australia'. Gorton pointed out that the ability to project power abroad did not, of itself, necessitate the stationing of forces overseas. If we did deploy them thus, it should be designed to strengthen the Australian fortress. The real issue was how best to defend Australian soil. It was this simple definition of Australia's interest that we were later to urge on David Fairbairn and William McMahon and over which they both stumbled and retreated. Moreover, when advocating cooperation with allies, Gorton seemed to be thinking of Asian countries. He did not mention ANZUS once.

With the case for withdrawing from Vietnam growing, and our troops in Singapore the subject of dispute over finance, this trimming of sails was expedient. Looking to the longer-term implications, we in the Defence Department saw some prospect of what in External Affairs I and others had long advocated in our advice, but without success—namely less dependence on the major powers in favour of what we came to call greater 'self-reliance'. But Gorton's ideas did not survive after his short-lived term as Defence Minister.

We saw less prospect of obtaining the Minister's support for our efforts to impose on the Services what we believed to be more rational priorities in respect of manpower and equipment. The Imperial Service Club speech offered the Services all that they said they needed—more spending, better conditions of service and (doubtless with the previous Minister in mind) loyalty from Ministers. There was nothing about facing up to the discipline of priorities.

I could see the Department and its programming system reverting to a role of simply supporting Service bids for funds—the 'adding machine' role of earlier times. I saw little prospect that Gorton would support increased authority for the Defence Minister over the Services, or any interest in reforming the existing clumsy apparatus of policy control. Before these gloomy ruminations materialised, Gorton was dismissed from the Cabinet by McMahon for reasons that had nothing to do with defence programming.

Fairbairn: Minister for Defence 1971

David Fairbairn took office in August 1971. He had won his Distinguished Flying Cross serving in the Air Force in Europe and had been Minister for Air as well as occupying some other portfolios during his career. Working for Ministers who disliked their predecessor, as did both Gorton and Fairbairn (and Hasluck in External Affairs), taught me to be wary of carrying personal loyalty to a Minister beyond the duties of the job, although in one or two cases a friendship was sustained when we were both in private life.

Fairbairn was a different personality from Gorton, and he was different in intellectual grasp of issues, ability to articulate ideas, speed of comprehension and much else. The Department found him congenial and no doubt the Services did even more so. He clearly enjoyed his official and social engagements with them. One noticed that he showed unusual respect for some senior officers, under whom he had served but to whom he was now entitled to issue firm orders. To the Department he was gentlemanly in conduct, invariably courteous and singularly undemanding. His reading of papers was rather slow. He left in doubt whether he always absorbed what the Department put to him.

According to Gorton, Fairbairn had earlier asked him for the High Commissionership in London. (After his Defence years he was to achieve the lesser post of Ambassador to the Netherlands.) He had the necessary social attributes for diplomatic life.

After the customary briefing of a new Minister into the various classified areas, it was necessary to explain the budget provisions that had already been announced. For the Department, after the disruptions of previous months, it was necessary to undertake the first effective effort to construct a five-year comprehensive programme and to establish what objectives we would recommend for the force structure now that the withdrawal of forces from the Vietnam commitment could be anticipated.

The Department needed more systems analysts. This was a relatively new concept in Canberra administration, especially in financial control, and analysts were hard to find. In any case there was some reluctance to enter the relatively unknown 'military' environment with its known tensions. For work on assessing the strategic environment I turned to Foreign Affairs. I brought in R.N. Hamilton after his service in Africa. Gordon Jockel took over the Joint Intelligence Organisation after serving as Ambassador in Indonesia, and later in 1973 I persuaded W.B. (Bill) Pritchett to join after serving in London. (He eventually became my successor as Secretary.) Paul Dibb, who later earned high repute for groundbreaking work on the force structure, came into the Joint Intelligence Organisation.

I came to the view that the Chief Defence Scientist was not making much impact on force structure debates and decisions. On the retirement of the current incumbent, I took the advice of the Chairman of the Commonwealth Scientific and Industrial Research Organisation (Sir Frederick White) and appointed to the position Dr John L. Farrands, head of the Aeronautical Research Laboratories. Added to his professional knowledge, he proved to have personal qualities of temperament that gave him persuasive influence in dealings with the Service Chiefs. My working relations with him were all the better for our sharing an addiction to fly-fishing on the stream adjoining my mountain property.

I wanted to develop the Defence Department's competence in assessing situations where we had a defence interest, notably Southeast Asia. I remained convinced that my old Department, Foreign Affairs (as External Affairs was renamed in 1970), should retain a large say in estimates and assessments of this kind, but I was aware of its limitations. I wanted some analysts to be closer to the realities of our military capabilities and the restraints on deployments overseas. Liaison officers from Foreign Affairs rotating through Canberra lacked this awareness. But several such officers, after being employed inside Defence alongside the military staff, provided a needed continuity of balanced judgement.

I needed this for the further reason that there was an overweighting of military judgement in the Department. While at the senior level we had the talented and wise Gordon Blakers, the lower levels were weaker. Civilians were needed to balance military judgement because there was evidence that some military officers' appreciations of the nature and whereabouts of threats was influenced by the role they saw for the Service whose uniform they wore. The Fairhall/Bland exhortation for complete objectivity could not always prevail over the pursuit of 'crest of the wave' technology pressed on the Services by British, American and other manufacturers.

To hold up Service bids for questioning was a heavy responsibility. In these early months the Department's staff did not always perform well. Apart from this form of supervision, the Department was also required to satisfy Service needs, where support functions had been centralised. Performance by the Department's computer services ran into difficulties, compounded by the loss of key personnel in an increasingly competitive environment. The Air Force was dissatisfied with the service. Keeping aircraft airworthy and in service depended on timely access to accurate records of its vast inventory.

We were in a continuous contest over the exercise of the authority that the Department claimed under the new programming procedures. Past Ministerial exhortations and claims of authority were not very effective in the face of a legal position that gave Service Ministers and their boards autonomy, other than control of the aggregates in the annual budget. In practice, the Defence Minister's strength lay in his conviction, persistence and courage rather than in past declarations. His standing in the Ministry and interested sections of the backbench no doubt contributed as well. He had no practical control of the nature and purpose of Service training (all Service activity when not in combat). Training reflected the Services' own expectations of where they would be fighting, although this was the prerogative of government. Beach landings, jungle tactics, air superiority or air-to-surface attack, destruction of submarines—all involved strategic assumptions that might or might not be valid or common to the three Services, about where we would find an enemy. Civilian control of running costs rested with Service Departmental Secretaries. They had no part in the formulation of strategic guidance, and might never have seen the Defence Committee's conclusions. I formed the impression that those Service Chiefs who took part in Defence Committee deliberations did not pass papers far down the command chain. My growing frustration appears in a diary note made on 26 September 1972:

> We are told by Army and Air, because of the complexity and number of people involved, they cannot, in less than six months, give us the statement of their long term capability objective and the contribution made (to it) by this (1973–8) Five Year Defence Programme. This after Army has written hundreds of pages calling for an Army of 50 000; the three Services proposed weapons authorisations of $3000 million (and were granted $1500m); and the three Chiefs and the three Secretaries endorsed in the Defence Administration Committee the need to spend some $7000m. in the next five years at fixed prices. In pursuit of what we ask? They claim time to answer.

This note, written some months before Labor re-wrote our strategic priorities, contained my own thinking on that matter:

> The transition to a defence policy for the Australian continent and its interests, away from having capabilities to offer loyalty to an ally, requires great mental adjustment—as well as perception and leadership of thought. There has not been much of the latter in the Defence Department (sic). We still don't know whether the Australian community really wants to spend money for the defence of Australia's interests. It is a new thought—at least since the threat of Japanese hegemony—which left curiously little mark except a belief in 'forward defence'.

Speaking to the Strategic and Defence Studies Centre at The Australian National University in 1974, I described the situation in 1972 as follows:

> The formalities of separate identity—sanctified by the Administrative Order—imposed an obstacle to the harmonising of Service activities, and to the reconciliation of the exercise of military command with the policy objectives of the Defence Minister—strategic, diplomatic, political, industrial, social, and (use of) resources. Communication inside the system was inadequate. It was formal, stilted, slow, and clumsy; too many people to get together.
>
> I, personally, was dismayed at the amount of time and nervous energy that had to be applied to enquiring—in terms acceptable (given the formal autonomy that existed)—into what was going on, whether what one read in the newspapers was true or not. Sometimes, if one called a committee together to consult or explore, one had to expect an argument as to whether there should be such a committee or what its terms of reference should be.
>
> ... For its part, the Department of Defence set out to break down the separatism by setting goals that its own staffing did not enable it to reach. The result was some frustration, thwarted single Service projects, and not enough suggested by way of alternatives promptly enough by the Central machinery.

A strong-minded Chairman of the Chiefs of Staff Committee, aided by such an influential civilian as Gordon Blakers, could bring about change in Service priorities for capital equipment (weapons and their platforms, such as ships and aircraft). Blakers has lately reminded me that in the mid-1960s Air Chief Marshal Sir Frederick Scherger, as Chairman of the Chiefs of Staff Committee, had brought about a preference for long-range maritime aircraft over bombers. He also overcame the Army's plan to locate a new task force on the Mornington Peninsula in the extreme (and salubrious) southeast of Australia, and had it despatched to north Queensland. More *Hercules* aircraft entered the programme. These were early signs of greater emphasis on continental defence, no doubt precipitated by the growing unpredictability of Sukarno's Indonesia. But in later times military advice of this kind, founded on strategic considerations rather than on the simpler notion of replacing what we already had in service, became rarer.

The Services liked deployments to overseas bases and the equipment that went with them. For the Navy, it was a 'blue-water' capability protected by carrier-borne aircraft that gave them status with the American and British navies. Air Force Chiefs described service at the base at Butterworth in Malaysia as good for morale, not merely for the operational exercises but also for families able to enjoy amenities not found around Australian airfields. I do not know whether these benefits coloured the belief that these deployments improved the likelihood of American support under ANZUS should we need it.

As to that, I retained a memory of the blunt warning that I heard Dean Rusk give to Hasluck in 1964. During the discussion of worsening relations between Malaysia and Indonesia, Hasluck volunteered to inform the Americans before committing Australian forces in support of Malaysia. Responding to the inherent assumption that such a deployment would trigger an expectation of American military support, Rusk pointedly said that the United States would expect that Australia would have introduced conscription and full mobilisation, and added 'there is no residuum of responsibility falling on the United States that is reached at a certain point'. This statement of the unpredictability of American military support confirmed to me how misleading had been many of the Australian Government's statements of the previous two decades, implying that ANZUS gave us an unqualified undertaking. Menzies had said: 'Australia cannot stand alone.' The truth of the matter had always been that in some circumstances, or for some testing period, Australian combat forces would stand alone. Some advisers, including myself, believed the Government should say as much. But the expediency of presenting the Coalition as the assurance of security for Australia, while it claimed that the Labor Party was distrusted in Washington, meant that such candour would be rejected as 'downgrading' ANZUS—a phrase frequently used.

When the Government told us in 1972 to prepare a White Paper on defence, we saw an opportunity to present new ideas and a more realistic view of what we needed to do for ourselves in response to the kind of threat-level then foreseeable.

The Department's 1972 'Defence Review': New ideas

Preparation of the White Paper required many contributors. R.N. Hamilton and Gordon Blakers, along with contributors from Foreign Affairs, did most of the drafting. I personally put my stamp on it by incorporating ideas that had matured in my mind over the years, some of which I described earlier. One of these was to obtain a changed expression of national attitude in statements of our strategic outlook. I wanted to have self-reliance recognised as having a necessary place in the posture of an independent self-respecting country. While in later decades the concept became regularly used in the language of all political parties, I believe I was the first to make it part of the language of discussion. Much defence policy lies in the mind; and what may seem no more than a slogan can be made a powerful directing influence on more material matters.

In a talk with the editor of a Sydney periodical [Donald Horne of the *Bulletin*], I tried out the idea that this concept might provide an escape from the sterile political argument between 'forward' and 'continental' defence.[24] I had noticed that Gorton had gone in that direction in a speech several months earlier. Each of the political parties had adopted one of the two concepts and the result had been an anaesthetising effect on discussion as to what best served Australia. 'Self-reliance' had an emotive resonance for people who took pride in the history and legends of the sturdy individualism of the country's early settlers and in past military campaigns—all of which shaped the ethos of the nation. We peppered our paper with references to self-reliance. It was the nearest I ever got to launching a political idea that might detach Australian policy statements from the degree of public dependence on the United States that had been expressed since 1950. Slogan or not, it would give defence planners something to replace the loose guidance calling for interoperability with the forces of our chief protector as the major objective. The draftsmen gave their draft a nationalist tone without unrealistically disassociating us from allies, declaring the protection of Australian interests (not simply the continent) to be the supreme objective of defence planning. On the stationing of forces overseas—a subject of sharp political debate—we wanted the Government's paper to recite some of the conditions which had to exist to permit maintenance of the deployment. The review suggested that deployment needed to satisfy the interests of both countries, which might not continue to be the case. Moreover the document could serve another purpose, which was to demonstrate the significance of distance, whether in estimating a threat or calculating the practicalities of deploying to meet it. There had long been imprecision as to what were the boundaries of 'our region', a term so frequently used in External Affairs and by Ministers.

One of my fetishes in the Defence Department was to have maps of Australia in plain view during discussions to show how remote we were from the mainland of Southeast Asia. The other side of that coin was the illustration of just how much distance separated our major defence bases in southern Australia from the area of assumed threat, even after the move northward had begun to take effect. The inclusion in the Defence Review of a map illustrating the distances in the continent's environment was in no sense an academic exercise.

Distance meant different things to different Services. In a pre-Vietnam War presentation in 1963 by the then Minister of how the Services saw their roles, the Air Force seemed to have recognised the constraints of distance, most of its airfields and maintenance facilities being in the south of the continent. Its primary function, the statement said, was 'the security of Australian territory and its sea and air approaches but with mobility to operate in Southeast Asia'. The Navy was unconstrained by distance so long as it had blue-water capabilities. It said its role 'was preparation for any kind of war in which Australia could be involved' and 'protection of convoys to the operational area wherever it may be'—Delphic but logical and a case for a blue-water navy until it was told otherwise. That came later when the Government declared a need for coastal protection in brown water by patrol boats. This revealed the paucity of ports and facilities in the north of Australia. For the Army, distance had always been a constraint when called on by governments to operate at a far distance (Japan, Korea, Vietnam and Malaysia), because of the paucity of means of transport for men and materiel.

Another powerful influence on the make-up of defence preparation was the immediacy (as distinct from the location) of the threat which the Government recognised and to which it expected the Services to respond. A threat would naturally cause the Services to ask for more resources; and experience showed that a more likely consequence, after governments predictably declined to do so, would be to absorb more of the Defence vote on stores and stockpiles and other consumables at the expense of capital assets in the form of equipment and ground installations for use in future contingencies. The current trend in the disposition of defence money led us to draw attention to this requirement of sound planning.[25] The new Five Year Defence Programme revealed that there would be inescapable expenditures in the future as obsolescence overtook major items (such as destroyers and aircraft), and illustrated the need to avoid cuts in current capital spending that would result in an overload on future budgets.

On the central question as to where our essential strategic interest lay, we pointed to the prospect of governments in Southeast Asia becoming more capable of dealing with their insurgencies and any likely defence problem. We recommended a changed strategic focus to one closer to our own territory. In this we were, I believe, tacitly acknowledging the past unwillingness of governments to have a defence vote big enough to enable us to project significant forces far from Australia. We argued for having capabilities 'which are particularly suitable to meet conditions in an ocean and archipelago environment'. This geographic definition would be a calculated retreat from giving priority to the Asian mainland to giving priority to an area containing the uncertainties that existed over Indonesia and Papua New Guinea. The argument had obvious implications for the Air Force and the Navy, giving them priority over the Army but weakening the case for a blue-water fleet based on a carrier, as compared with other naval vessels. The Army's Chief had difficulty in accepting the priority.

After its finalisation, the Prime Minister threw the status of the document into confusion by deciding against presenting it as a White Paper expressing Government policy, and instead declaring it to be a Departmental 'Review'. When Fairbairn presented it to Parliament, his speech accepted the idea of greater self-reliance. He was probably thinking of hardware rather than attitude. He was more equivocal on the question of retaining forces overseas.

In effect, the Department was lumbered with responsibility for a hybrid—a document that included views we knew the Government would want to include which we did not share, and an analysis of the desirable strategic posture that failed to receive government endorsement. We were chided by the Opposition for being 'political' in our advice. Nevertheless, the Labor Opposition (and specifically a future Prime Minister, Paul Keating) gave much of the 'Review' a tick of approval. From the backbench Gorton liked the attempt to remove the artificial dichotomy between 'forward' and 'continental' defence.

McMahon's caution might well have been for fear of devil in the detail. In retrospect I believe I made an error in allowing the document to include every new idea that the Department felt to be important. It became an indigestible document for Ministers. I doubt whether the document had any lasting influence on members of the Coalition Cabinet or of its backbench. Domestically, it did disseminate ideas within the Services and the Department that might have influenced Service priorities. But this can only be speculation.

The 'Review' has not received much attention by historians or by commentators on the defence policies of the 1970s, but those interested in the evolution of thinking in Canberra's advisory system will recognise that much of the document presaged reforms later implemented in the Whitlam/Barnard years. Herein may lie the reason why, as we shall see, Labor, when taking office in 1972, found the Department well prepared to implement its policies.

While preparing the intended White Paper, we found that Fairbairn was more comfortable in discussing Service bids for equipment than in more abstract reasoning over the strategic outlook. In this there was a contrast with the visiting Defence Minister of the Federal Republic of Germany, Helmut Schmidt. Fortuitously, as a result of an unexpected commitment in the House of Representatives which prevented Fairbairn keeping an appointment with him, I was called upon to receive Schmidt. I called together the members of the Defence Committee (the Service Chiefs and the Secretaries of the Departments of the Prime Minister, Foreign Affairs and Treasury). It proved to be a most stimulating experience. Schmidt gave us his view of the state of Europe and of the Western alliance in the stand-off with the Soviet Union. He asked all the right questions after I offered my view of the situation in Northeast Asia and, more confidently, the prospects in Southeast Asia and in Australia's neighbourhood. We were privileged because Schmidt later became Chancellor of the German Federation and earned the reputation of being foremost among the European statesmen of modern times.

It was the more regrettable that Fairbairn fluffed his opportunity, when toasting him at an official dinner, by making lame jokes about the Iron Cross on his visitor's aircraft and the superfluity of a party in a democracy having to proclaim the word 'democratic' in the title of his political party. Schmidt replied with an urbane account of the honourable history of his party in outlasting three dictators (including Adolf Hitler).

Attention to ongoing matters for decision did not wait on the outcome of the Defence Review. Decisions were needed on the acquisition of a new type of destroyer for the Navy and on the development of a naval base at Garden Island, south of Fremantle. There was a strong push from the Navy's designers and dockyards within the system to have the destroyer's hull designed and built in Australia. As the Navy intended to incorporate from overseas the most modern (and changing) sensors, weapons and control systems, there were warnings that matching them with the hull would be a formidable and perhaps insuperable task. Nevertheless, the plan received Defence Committee endorsement. I did not feel I had the necessary understanding of the subject to deny what the Navy wanted. As time passed, the problems grew, the list of requirements grew, the size of the hull grew, and so did the estimates of cost.

During the year I took opportunities to escape Canberra and to learn about Service life, albeit in pampered and peaceful conditions. In March the Navy winched me down to HMAS *Brisbane*'s after-deck from a helicopter at sea during a Pacific Ocean exercise, enabling me to observe a *Tartar* missile firing. They then tested my nerves with a jackstay transfer across the ocean waves to HMAS *Parramatta*. In this my safety from being doused in the sea seemed to depend on what the crew members, who were holding taut the hawser, thought of this particular civilian.

Some time later the Army, during a visit to their training establishment at Singleton, had me throwing grenades at targets, followed by an unscheduled lesson in helicopter flying. On my return flight to Victoria Barracks the obliging Army pilot offered me the controls, assuring me that his status as instructor made this legal. I headed south erratically over the Central Coast aiming, on his instruction, at the Sydney Harbour Bridge in a long descent. But the prospect of disaster as we approached tall buildings beyond the bridge caused a collapse of nerve and I asked to be relieved of my post.

The Services, particularly the Army, have a good record of preserving the historic buildings they have occupied since colonial days. But there were eyesores in the form of structures erected through necessity in environmentally sensitive areas during the Second World War. At this time in the 1970s there was not much interest in the environment among politicians. As a former Sydney-sider I took a possibly parochial interest in Sydney Harbour. I visited several sites where there were offending structures. I questioned whether the Army needed, for any operational purpose, sites on headlands adjacent to the harbour in Sydney; and in particular the wooden barracks resembling woolsheds disfiguring a site of such historic importance as South Head. Having achieved their removal I took a more sympathetic view of the Navy's claim to be by the sea, but helped ensure that when they were provided with an installation for advanced training on South Head it would be secreted underground.

In the same mood I had cast a speculative eye on the Navy's ugly industrial stockpile littering part of historic Garden Island. This was the forerunner of some rehabilitation of historic buildings, which the Navy had preserved well. When Labor was in office, soon afterwards, they transferred most of the materials to an abandoned car factory at Zetland so that the Navy had quick access.

By October, the defeat of the Government in the forthcoming election was widely predicted. There were many activities and international arrangements needing to be carried on, irrespective of which political party was in power. Few on Labor's front bench had experience in government. Allies would need reassurance that classified military information entrusted to Australia would be protected. In the debate on the Defence Review, Lance Barnard, Labor's Defence spokesman, had declared his party's opposition to foreign bases on Australian soil, and their intention to withdraw from Singapore. I asked Fairbairn for permission to meet Barnard in order to assure him that he would be fully briefed on such matters immediately, should he gain office, and to advise him to hold off definitive public commitments until he was in possession of all the relevant information. I said there would be nothing prejudicial to the Coalition in anything I said to Barnard.

Fairbairn was liberal-minded and forthcoming in response. In a discussion with Barnard over lunch at Parliament House I told him that we would be ready with information if elected. He told me of various policy changes that Labor had in mind. One of them was to centralise the Defence Group of Departments along with their control. I said that he would find that I had some definite views on that subject to offer him.

In November, on the recommendation of Coombs, I attended a seminar at Ditchley in England, held by an Atlantic club interested in international affairs. There was a mixture of senior American and British officials, academics of both countries, and members of the Armed Services Committee of Congress and the White House staff. Outside the meeting the Director of the Royal College of Defence Studies, Alistair Buchan, told me that the shift of British interest towards Europe was increasing the competition for places at the college from Europeans and reducing the interest in the strategic significance of Australia's neighbourhood, with implications for the number of places offered to Australia. He believed we should create our own Defence Studies College.

Final months of McMahon's Coalition Government

It became clear as the months went by that the McMahon Government had become hostage to its doctrinal attachment to 'forward defence' and to the associated deployments in Malaysia and Singapore. This was exploited by the Democratic Labor Party in particular, but also by an opportunistic Singapore Government. That Government had earlier demanded rent for premises occupied by the Australians sent to defend them, as well as reciprocal use of bases in Australia. When McMahon visited the two countries in June 1972, with an election imminent, his mind remained in Australia. His principal interest seemed to be to obtain a public affirmation, from his hosts, for use with the Australian media who accompanied him in the aircraft and others back in Australia, that both countries wanted our forces for the present. He seemed a rattled man. He stumbled repeatedly while recording an interview for a Sydney radio station, with John Bunting (the Secretary of the Prime Minister's Department) and I doing our best to point out his misstatements of facts or policy. He was good-natured to his advisers and did not mind being corrected.

During the return flight, while the Prime Minister spent time at the back of the aircraft with the media, I recorded in my diary:

> Australia is now governed in almost continuous press conference. No discussion of substance about the purpose or consequences on a matter of foreign policy or external defence in this part of the world seems possible without reference to how the press in Australia will react.

McMahon was like a bird hopping from branch to branch over a loaded gun.

He was invariably considerate to me. We met informally on occasions. I often met Ministers at funerals burying their departed colleagues. On such an occasion, and others, McMahon said he regretted being outwitted ('kept in the dark', as he put it) in his wish to appoint me as Secretary when he had the Foreign Affairs portfolio. But I could not honestly reciprocate his admiration.

In my area of administration there was drift and frustration. On 27 October I entered in my diary:

> The past week has seen some cases of an unnecessarily large number of senior executives—in our case two Generals and myself—pursuing enquiries or waiting about while more urgent problems burned because of a ... lack of a sense of the importance of things, the addiction to trivia, and the plain confusion of mind which fails to communicate promptly and clearly.

I suggested to Fairbairn that he should move to establish a review of the organisation of the Defence Group of Ministers and Departments. Not surprisingly, he said that McMahon would not want to open up such a controversial matter. After Labor's victory was announced on the night of Saturday 2 December 1972, I obtained Fairbairn's approval to give Barnard his classified briefing at his earliest convenience. Even though uncertain as to the policies I would be implementing (if still in the job), I recorded in my diary my relief at escaping from months of frustration and unproductive effort.

ENDNOTES

1 This probably refers to a memoir that Tange began writing. At his death he had written only a few draft passages.

2 That is, the Government in which John Gorton was Prime Minister and Malcolm Fraser was Minister for Defence. Tange sometimes used the term Ministry in referring to a government in a way that is more common in Britain than in Australia.

3 See, for example, Peter Edwards with Gregory Pemberton, *Crises and Commitments: The Strategy and Diplomacy of Australia's Involvement in Southeast Asian Conflicts 1948-65*, Allen & Unwin with the Australian War Memorial, St Leonards, NSW, 1992, pp. 53–56; and David Horner, *Defence Supremo: Sir Frederick Shedden and the making of Australian defence policy*, Allen & Unwin, St Leonards, NSW, 2000, pp. 259–60, 268–70, 286 and 288.

4 See Desmond Ball and David Horner, *Breaking the Codes: Australia's KGB network 1944-50*, Allen & Unwin, St Leonards, NSW, 1998.

5 Robert O'Neill, *Australia in the Korean War 1950–53, volume 1, Strategy and Diplomacy*, Australian War Memorial and Australian Government Publishing Service, Canberra, 1981.

6 It has not proved possible to identify this document in published sources, such as Roger Holdich, Vivianne Johnson, Pamela Andre (eds), *The ANZUS Treaty 1951*, Department of Foreign Affairs and Trade, Canberra, 2001.

7 Tange had two children, Christopher (b. 1944) and Jennifer (b. 1947).

8 This is presumably a reference to O'Neill, *Australia in the Korean War 1950–53, volume 1*, and Edwards, *Crises and Commitments: The Strategy and Diplomacy of Australia's Involvement in Southeast Asian Conflicts 1948-65*. See also Horner, *Defence Supremo: Sir Frederick Shedden and the making of Australian defence policy*.

9 Tange later recorded that the Minister who had said this to Barwick was Sir John McEwen, Deputy Prime Minister and Minister for Trade.

10 Tange did not discover until the publication of *Crises and Commitments* in 1992 that the Prime Minister's Department had been critical of the External Affairs Department's handling of policy towards Indonesia at the time of Confrontation.

11 See Garry Woodard, *Asian Alternatives: Australia's Vietnam Decision and Lessons on Going to War*, Melbourne University Press, Carlton, 2004, chapter 10, (pp. 191–208), and Edwards, *Crises and Commitments: The Strategy and Diplomacy of Australia's Involvement in Southeast Asian Conflicts 1948-65*, pp. 335–40.

12 The house guest was Tange's daughter, Jennifer.

13 Tange was referring to London, Washington and Tokyo. The first career appointment as Ambassador in Washington was made in 1964.

14 *Commonwealth Parliamentary Debates*, vol. H of R 66, 10 March 1970, pp. 232–47.

15 Statement made by Kim Beazley to Parliament on 14 October 1988.

16 Sir Henry Bland, 'Some aspects of defence administration in Australia', Roy Milne Lecture 1970 (published as a pamphlet by the Australian Institute of International Affairs). See also Fedor A. Mediansky, 'Defence Reorganisation 1957–75', in William J. Hudson (ed.), *Australia in World Affairs 1971–1975*, George Allen & Unwin, North Sydney, 1980, pp. 37–64.

17 This comment was written before the publication of David Horner, *Strategic Command: General Sir John Wilton and Australia's Asian Wars*, Oxford University Press, South Melbourne, 2005.

18 Ian McNeill, 'General Sir John Wilton: A Commander for his Time', in David Horner (ed.), *The Commanders: Australian military leadership in the twentieth century*, George Allen & Unwin, Sydney, 1984, pp. 316–34.

19 This is probably a reference to the passage (including extensive quotations from Fraser) in Philip J. Ayres, *Malcolm Fraser: a biography*, William Heinemann, Richmond, Vic., 1987.

20 William C. Battle was the American Ambassador to Australia from July 1962 to August 1964.

21 On this episode, see the accounts in Ayres, *Malcolm Fraser: a biography*; Ian Hancock, *John Gorton: he did it his way*, Hodder Headline, Sydney, 2002; and Peter Edwards, *Arthur Tange: Last of the Mandarins*, Allen & Unwin, St Leonards, NSW, 2006.

22 See the discussion of Fraser's style in Patrick Weller, *Malcom Fraser PM: a study in prime ministerial power*, Penguin, Ringwood, Vic., 1989.

[23] A summary of Gorton's speech of 18 June 1971 to the Imperial Service Club in Sydney was published as John Gorton, '"Forward defence" or "fortress Australia"?', *Sydney Morning Herald*, 21 June 1971. The speech and its significance are discussed in Hancock, *John Gorton: he did it his way*, pp. 343–45.

[24] Horne recounted this meeting as follows: 'Arthur Tange came to my office, sat in a remote chair, forcibly immobile, like a statue of a nineteenth-century statesman in a frock coat, and asked me if I had a new phrase that could replace 'Forward Defence'. *'Fortress Australia?'—never. 'Self-reliance?'—perhaps.'* Donald Horne, *Into the Open*, HarperCollins, Sydney, 2000, p. 156 (emphasis in original).

[25] A note indicates that Tange intended to insert some statistics at this point, to illustrate his point. There is no indication of the particular statistics that he intended to insert.

Chapter 2

Labor in Office

Labor's policies

Within hours of the announcement on Saturday 2 December 1972 of Labor's majority in the House of Representatives, I spoke by telephone to my new Minister, Lance Barnard, in Launceston. He said he wanted me to continue in office to assist him. Whitlam arranged with the Governor-General that he and Barnard would share between them all the portfolios as a temporary measure pending the Senate results, which would enable a full caucus to be formed to elect the full Ministry.

In contrast with the vacuum in policy-making and the politically defensive attention to trivia that had characterised the last months of the McMahon Government, Labor deluged us with policy objectives and organisational changes. In the first weeks the auspices were good for someone in Defence wanting to serve the new Government's policy with enthusiasm. I believed that I understood their central defence policies, some of which I had long been advocating to their predecessors with little success. But I could not know Labor's intentions, as distinct from rhetoric, in respect of the American connection. I was uncertain as to how the Ministers in office would handle publicly declared policies of disclosing, or possibly terminating, the activities of the United States in the facilities shared with Australia at Pine Gap and Nurrungar. I hoped to dissuade the Ministers from either course when they were given the facts to which, under the strict rules that had been established by previous governments, they had not been made privy when in Opposition.

Having spent Sunday looking over papers prepared on various changes predicted by Labor, I took them to Barnard in Parliament House on Monday. Shortly afterwards Whitlam joined the discussion, which picked up some matters from my meeting with Barnard in October. Both declared that they would look to me to help achieve Labor's priorities.

In that first meeting the Ministers said they wanted the Service Departments abolished and the Services put under the control of the Defence Minister. Without any prompting the Prime Minister said he wanted me to use my authority to achieve this for the Minister. My diary records that in the conversation Barnard said he wanted to strengthen the role of civilian advice. When he went on to say that he wanted to delegate more to the Department I counselled caution, because there would be sensitivities in the Services.

It was the beginning of a very busy three months. In my area of interest the Government was encouraging and forward-looking. In that first week I was given more policy directions than in the 21 months since Fraser had left the Gorton Government. I (and other senior officers in Defence) did not suffer the debilitating distrust of some of Whitlam's Ministers towards their Departments. Although Whitlam was giving most attention to foreign policy changes of a declaratory nature that did not require approval by Cabinet or Parliament, neither of which had yet met, he also spent time on Defence matters because of the interconnection. He called me in on several occasions to hear progress.

In response to the stated intention of the two Ministers to reform the fragmented Defence system, I had recommended that, before legislation could be prepared for a merger after a necessary inquiry, Barnard should be given all three Service portfolios. I also said he should continue to hold them after a new Ministry had been formed because, if other Ministers were appointed, his continued control of the Services would be lost.

Due to the workload, I recommended that the Supply Department be placed *pro tem* under another Minister, with whom Defence could rely on continued good cooperation. However, on this aspect Barnard thought otherwise, citing his interest in controlling the Defence factories and their large workforce.

Other matters requiring urgent attention were the cessation of National Service, and the notification to allies of the intended withdrawal of ground forces from Asia. Various senior officers were involved in these tasks, particularly the Secretary of the Army Department, the experienced Bruce White, and one of my deputies, Eric Dwyer. To inform Whitlam without delay of the nature and purpose of the joint facilities in which the Americans were involved fell to me, assisted by the Chief Defence Scientist, Dr John L. Farrands, who could speak with authority on the operations. Almost two hours were spent answering the Prime Minister's questions. We stated our view of the global importance of their activities, given the then state of relations between the Soviet Union and the Western allies, as well as their other beneficial capabilities.

These various encounters with the country's new leaders led me to confide to my diary some enthusiastic sentiments about the prospects of 'changes to come, ideas, constructive ideas, attacks on some myths behind which shoddy ideas and careerism have been sheltered by conservative Ministers and the active backbench'. These bottled-up sentiments, expressed in the purple prose that comes naturally late at night after an exhausting day, did not spring from any partisan adherence on my part to the Labor side of politics. Working at different levels under the Curtin, Chifley, Menzies, Gorton and McMahon Governments, I had tried to understand policy without being passionate about party success or failure.

My enthusiasm for the new regime was soon tempered when we experienced in the first months the lack of concerns for confidentiality, rejection of the system of security clearances, undisciplined public trespass by Ministers outside their portfolio, and unwillingness or inability to control free-ranging Ministerial staff.

Labor's reforms had to be fitted into the ongoing management of the Services, and satisfaction of the daily requirements which do not wait upon changes of government. Barnard had to cope with a deluge of decisions, while fending off attacks on him from Labor's left. He had still to absorb the content of the current year's defence programme and the forward projections into which any changes would have to be fitted. We had to caution him against making changes in a hurry before the consequences were understood—for example, acquiring new fighter aircraft while the *Mirages* were still serviceable. There were election promises that had to be implemented, such as the improved pay and conditions recommended by Justice Woodward, along with some welcome industrial principles for deciding these matters.

We felt ourselves fortunate to have an industrious and congenial Minister, who sought advice from civilian and Service officers and who refrained from premature announcements of decisions affecting Australia's allies. This contrasted with the actions of some of his colleagues, who were addressing démarches to foreign ambassadors or publishing denunciations in language offensive to American leaders. On 30 December I remarked in my diary (in mixed metaphors) that 'men unused to power flex their muscles, and crow like victorious cocks'. Moreover, after we gave our sobering advice the Defence vote was spared the spending frenzy spreading elsewhere, in the absence of Parliament and of any effective Treasurer's control. As my diary recorded: '"Come and get it" is ringing out of Ministerial offices.'

Principles of pay-fixing got short shrift from some Ministers as they demanded high salaries for personal staff. At the same time the salaries of all departmental Secretaries were put on the same levels, presumably reflecting the demand for equality among Ministers. We had the bizarre result of the Secretary to the Treasury and the Secretary of Defence receiving the same pay as the Secretary of the new and insignificant Department of the Media.

To bring about many of the changes, I handed responsibility to other senior officers. Their numbers were not large. They had assistance from the Joint Military Staff under Rear Admiral Bill Dovers. Manpower decisions were handled by a deputy secretary, Eric Dwyer (who had been brought in earlier from the Public Service Board) and by the three members of the Service Boards responsible for personnel. Farrands (who later was to be appointed head of a Department of his own) was put in charge of preparation for negotiating changes at the US–Australian joint facilities. Financial programming under our unique 'rolling' system was in the hands of Matt Hyland. His task was to devise an integrated system applicable after the separate Departments had been abolished. Intelligence assessments for the new strategic review were provided by Gordon Jockel, formerly a senior Foreign Affairs officer. He was aided by Paul Dibb who, a decade later, was to make a major impact on the force structure under Minister Kim Beazley.

I retained for myself the last word on the new strategic assessments for the Government and in addition, in consultation with the Chairman of the Chiefs of Staff Committee, Admiral Sir Victor Smith, coordinated what was being served up to Barnard.

Various international discussions also fell to me as early as the last week before Christmas 1972 when Whitlam included me in his visit to New Zealand to meet their new Labour Prime Minister, Norman Kirk. That journey had an unintended consequence. Over the Tasman Sea, the Air Force's BAC-111 lost one of its two engines with a ruptured turbine. We limped slowly back to Fairbairn. During the silence in the cabin that followed the ominous jolt that shook the aircraft, when I and others were silently studying the height of the waves not far below, our ex-Air Force Prime Minister seemed to be enjoying himself, making quips up and down the cabin. It was later decreed that the hazard to Ministers of trans-oceanic flights called for a four-engined Boeing 707 for the VIP flight. Its purchase was grafted on to the Defence programme, although it had no combat priority.

One task that I could not delegate was planning the review that I was to conduct into how best to integrate the Service Departments into Defence, along with the defence industries and science laboratories, to give the Minister for Defence effective control over the Services.

Consultations and plans for merging five Departments

In January 1973 I began preparing material for the announcement to be made by the Government as soon as Parliament met in late February. In addition, I needed riding instructions, in the form of terms of reference for the inquiry into the desired integration.

To gain support for Labor's intention Whitlam wished to publish the 1958 report of the Morshead Committee to the Menzies Government, which Labor believed had much the same objective as theirs in 1973. This led to a somewhat arcane discussion with the Cabinet Secretary, John Bunting, who explained the convention against Ministers being given access to the Cabinet records of its predecessor. Was the report a Cabinet document or not? Whatever the answer, Whitlam, with his sense of propriety, decided to obtain the approval of the Leader of the Opposition once he had been chosen.

The Government announced its defence reorganisation intentions in a statement made by Barnard (conjointly with the Prime Minister) on 19 December, only days after taking office. The statement of some 2000 words, which I had drafted, incorporated the Government's intention to spread the workload by appointing a person having Ministerial status in another portfolio as Minister Assisting the Minister for Defence (a course that I recommended). This clumsy and not wholly effective device to bring the load on a Minister to manageable proportions had been used by the Menzies Government in 1960 (on my advice on that occasion as well). Legal opinion had warned that the appointment within a portfolio of a second Minister enjoying emoluments might be found to be unconstitutional, in breach of Section 64 of the Constitution, with severe penalties under Section 44 (iv) for the Member of Parliament so appointed.

Barnard's press statement contained, in effect, the terms of reference that I wanted. It is publicly available, both in Hansard and in the Tange Report, and need not be reproduced here. In drafting it for the Minister I thought that he should, for several reasons, confine himself to broad objectives, avoiding precision about detailed organisation. Obviously any conclusions I might reach would have to follow consultation with those already experienced in the daily management of the activities of the Services and in the satisfaction of the essential requirements of each Service (and they differed).

Unlike defence policy-making, this had not been the function of my Department. Because the Services had the constant requirement of a steady morale in meeting current and potential deployment demands, they needed assurance that arbitrary solutions would not be imposed on them by a new and unfamiliar Labor Government, and that consultations would be real. Politically, the Government would need to safeguard itself in Parliament on these points.

The stated objectives were the creation of a single Department containing the staff of Defence and the Service Departments (the Department of Supply being left for further study, which accorded with my own request). The statement said each Service would retain its own identity and exercise substantial delegation of authority; some areas under single-Service control would be transferred into central functional management in the Department; there was to be more effective central military control of operations and related military activity; and there was to be improved presentation to Parliament of the contribution made to Defence by the activities of the Services, and their cost. In later years, as other agencies developed programming of the kind pioneered in Defence, this was to be labelled measurement of 'output'.

As the Ministers had accepted my draft, the words identified virtually everything that I had found deficient in the system in the previous three years. Approval by the new Government was encouraging and established a political signpost to the future.

How the statement was received in the Services I would learn only later. With their minds occupied with the redeployments and force reductions (in the

Army), along with the daily tasks of the units and formations around the country and abroad, including Vietnam, there was likely to be less attention than we gave it in the Department of Defence.

To start the process I called together the three Service Departmental Secretaries. They were Sam Landau (Navy), Bruce White (Army) and Fred Green (Air). I spent several weeks meeting them from time to time and seeking their views on the shape of the future. I wanted to know how they functioned in relation to their two-star colleagues in the Service Boards and much else, before meeting with the Service Chiefs.

I did not expect that the Government would want the inquiry to examine the command structures of the Services at the operational level, below the boards to which the Departmental Secretaries belonged. This would in any case have been outside my experience and competence.

Strategy for making the changes

Early in my consultations the Services had asked whether I would follow the experience of other countries. Apart from great disparities in size, I reacted firmly against this familiar lack of confidence in the ability of Australians to create machinery relevant to their own constitutional situation without running for tutelage from the mother country or any other. In any case the failure of the British to reform their system was attested to by a former Secretary of State for Defence and later Prime Minister, Harold Macmillan. It seemed that we had already made all Britain's mistakes.

In his book *At the End of the Day*, Macmillan said:

> The Act of Parliament which established the Ministry of Defence after the war clothed the Minister with doubtful authority and gave him insufficient means to fulfil even the functions which he was supposed to carry out.

The similarity in Australia was striking when he wrote:

> Their Lordships of the Admiralty, with their hierarchy of Admirals under the First Sea Lord; the War Office with its Secretary of State and Army Council; even the later-created Air Ministry again with its Secretary of State—it was in these historic bodies that rested the real, practical control. Moreover, the responsibility of their political heads to Parliament had scarcely been altered by the emergence of the Minister of Defence.

When he became Prime Minister, Macmillan was still frustrated. In 1957 he suggested to his Defence Minister, Duncan Sandys, the creation of a single integrated Defence Department. 'All through the spring of 1958 there was a kind of smouldering fire in Whitehall.' When a White Paper emerged in 1958 four separate Ministers remained. A Chief of Defence Staff was created, but on the basis that 'he was to have no control of his own'. Australia seems to have followed this course. In 1962 and 1963 Macmillan tried again. In 1964 a reorganisation established 'the principle' of functional organisations serving all three Services. But, on my observation years later, practice was different. His frustration led Macmillan to say in 1963: 'If we have to decide between two possible courses of action we must always choose the more radical.'

As I said earlier, I decided that gradualism rather than radical change was better for a new and inexperienced Labor Government. Others might think that the political judgement of the Prime Minister of Britain was better than mine. I do not remember any cries for swifter change when I was preparing my report. But there was plenty of opposition to the content of the changes.

Another British Minister, Alan Clark, had said publicly that in considering proposals that came to him for decisions on new weapons acquisitions, he would consider first to what extent approval would further the career of the applicant. I began with a less cynical view of the motives at work in our Services. But I wanted a system of testing that went wider than the operational preferences of the applicant Service.

Defining the general objectives was relatively easy; but a replacement organisation had to be one that could be worked cooperatively and efficiently by Service personnel accustomed to procedures unique to each Service wherever located throughout Australia and at overseas bases.

Gradualism would be needed to avoid any sharp break in the operational state of the Navy, Army and Air Force. It would not be possible to foresee every possible hitch, psychological or otherwise, that would affect the working together of the senior personnel of the three Services in their support of the operational commands. There would be a testing period for the acceptance by some of new lines of authority, and acquiescence in new sources of material support. It would be prudent to leave some areas untouched, at least for the present. Rather than looking for complete solutions to be handed down from above (or from outside as many in the Services might see the Defence Department), the better approach would be, in my judgement, to create new organisations in the Department, covering clustered functions, where rationalisation would become a self-generating process.

The work of the advisers, then and later, was essential to the reorganisation. We did not always agree. White, who knew the military way of looking at things better than I, warned me against, as he put it, 'opening war on too many fronts at once'. But, personal conviction apart, I had been given a deadline for satisfying a somewhat impetuous government's demand.

As to that, I had to make a judgement as to how far the Whitlam Ministers and Caucus would stand up to resistance that could be expected to any change

I might recommend. I could foresee the kind of opposition that some changes would draw from a core of members of Parliament likely to oppose any changes, particularly by a Labor Government; from the Returned and Services League, from the conservative press (fed by the disgruntled), and from the many who held a sceptical view of the competence of public servants, particularly if the much admired Services were to be made beholden to them in some respect. I would be under the disadvantage, on that emotional issue, of the seeming lack of awareness among them of the extent to which a conservative Menzies Government had in 1958 already endorsed the essential place of civilian Secretaries as one reason for rejecting the then proposal to abolish the Service Boards. Indeed, the same unawareness of the accepted role of civilians existed within the Services themselves, especially among personnel who were located at some distance from Russell in Canberra.

The task, essentially, was to find a form of public administration that would effectively support the military forces acting under Ministerial control in conformity with Government policy and under scrutiny of the amount and purpose of expenditures they incurred or committed for the future. I was not asked to share with any military officer the management of the inquiry, and still less that I carry the weight of a committee of three arguing about what areas I should or should not explore in an exercise in public administration in which I had accumulated some experience. I was simultaneously guiding an inexperienced Minister through plentiful problems and recurring crises.

I needed advisers who understood the constitutional and administrative principles to be embedded in the reformed system of Ministerial control. I arranged that I be assisted full time by Bruce White, whom I considered to be the most competent as well as the most experienced of the three Service Departmental Secretaries.

Abolition of the Service Boards: Reasons

Integration of control of policy into Defence was not possible if the Service Boards remained with the legal powers they possessed. Nor would it be possible to give effective command of the Services to the senior military officer so long as the legal authority of the Chiefs of Staff within each Service differed. In the Navy, executive command rested in the Naval Board and not with the Chief of Naval Staff. In the Army Department the Minister presided over the subordinate generals who were members of the Board. Since it is axiomatic that Ministerial decisions necessarily embrace some considerations that are never revealed—such as party considerations, electoral advantage, trade-offs within the Government and doubtless much else—the Army Minister adopted the device of absenting himself if he foresaw that a Board item was likely to be submitted to Cabinet.

Furthermore, the functions of some Board members would be lost, wholly or in part, to whatever new directors of common Service functions were set up in the reformed Defence Department, in accordance with the guiding principles.

As to accountability, the dispersion of authority among the 15 two-star officers and their three three-star Chiefs made it difficult to establish precisely who was accountable to the Minister for actions (or lack of them) in the Service. This was important when things went wrong. Not the least challenge would be the disappearance from the Board, after his Department was abolished, of the civilian carrying the traditional and legal powers of a Departmental Secretary. What would be necessary was to 'boil down', into a single formula applicable to all three Services, the existing relationships of Service officers and Secretaries. Much of my discussion with White, Landau and Green was directed to this idea and to the practicalities involved.

All the Secretaries agreed that continuing three separate systems of controlling expenditures and financial commitments, as required by the *Audit Act* and financial regulations, had to be rejected. In April I had set up a more formal system of consultation in the form of a Senior Consultative Committee, provided with investigating staff, to advise me. Bruce White was its leader. The Service Departmental Secretaries were charged with keeping the Chiefs of Staff informed on where the inquiry was going. By September several sticking points emerged.

Direct discussion—The Secretary and four Service Chiefs: Conclusions reached

While the Committee continued to meet—in about 17 meetings in all—I decided I should sit down with the four Chiefs and deal with them directly. My report describes the main matters that arose. In my discussions I gave way on some matters recommended to us. An example was the idea of moving the Service Chiefs of personnel into the Defence Department.

It was surprising that (as far as I recall) the Chiefs did not challenge my intention to continue to keep strategic assessments under departmental control; nor my intention to have departmental control of the staff examining Service equipment and manpower bids, to ensure their conformity to strategic need and to a balanced force structure. The challenge on the second was to build up and remain continuous, as I shall later record.

All the Chiefs had the right to go to the Minister with any complaints; as far as I know none did. It was helpful to me that my colleague as Chairman of the Chiefs of Staff Committee, Admiral Smith, was trusted by Barnard. I surmise that the absence of any complaint from him would have been reassuring to Barnard that Service interests were properly considered.

For the Chiefs a major recommendation, with which they all concurred, was that the chief military officer in the Department of Defence (already of superior rank) be given for the first time legal power of command over the three Services, while providing that the Chief of Staff of each Service would be responsible to the Minister 'through' the renamed Chief of Defence Force Staff. The single-Service Chief would be acknowledged as 'the professional head of his Service' and have command of it, subject to certain stipulations.

I took the opportunity to employ symbolism to reflect the concept that a common purpose must govern the activities of the three Services. I restored to usage the compendious title 'Australian Defence Force' which the 1915 *Defence Act* had declared to be composed of 'three arms'. Fraser's 1970 statement, for example, had not once used the term. In due course (after my time) the commander had his title changed to the unambiguous 'Chief of the Defence Force'.

With the Department now planned to contain a commander of all the Services, and the Service Departments and the Service Boards to be abolished, the three Departmental Secretaries (or Chief Officers) would disappear likewise. The *Audit Act*, and the many regulations stipulating financial controls, called for substitute appointments. The history of Defence administration and the known views of governments from both sides of politics clearly required that the function be vested in the sole remaining First Division public servant—the Secretary of the Department of Defence.

Whereas in each Service Board this officer operated in conjunction with a three-star Service Chief and four or five officers at two-star level, I had to propose an arrangement for relations between two individuals to share the administration of the Defence Force. Some questions of principle had to be disposed of. I had no hesitation in riding off course the idea that had previously surfaced in the Army of having the Chief of Defence Force Staff solely responsible for representing the Department to the Minister, converting a Department of State into a *de facto* military headquarters.

But the Secretary could no longer have his powers and duties identical with those of civilian Departments under the *Public Service Act*. Behind these organisational challenges lay some deep-seated tensions in some areas between civilians and Service officers carrying out their respective duties. I needed to recognise this in proposing the new administrative arrangements—a subject to which I shall return later.

In the discussions some Chiefs were more constructive (whether in support or in criticism) than others. One I went to see privately in his office to remind him that the Government's call for reforms in the system called for ideas and cooperation from him no less than from me.

Discussion gradually reduced the areas in contention. The Chiefs were reluctant to accept abolition of the Service Boards, even though achieving a commander of the Defence Force with access to the Defence Minister. I held to the view, already explained above, that their existence would be inconsistent with the new line of command and, in addition, obscured accountability. Most accepted the idea when they were reassured that there would be no objection to their setting up their own advisory committees, when the Chief assumed direct responsibility for activities previously controlled by their two-star officers and for which they had been accountable to the Service Board.

There were reservations (particularly from the Air Force) about my concept of some Service officers being appointed to serve under the Secretary in policy positions in a 'two-hatted' arrangement—responsible to the Secretary in respect of financial and other policy directions, and to his Service Chief in respect of his operational priorities. One example I proposed was in the area of supply. Another concerned the construction activities of the Services in their bases, ports, airfields and training establishments. I argued that being answerable to two persons was already a fact in the Services. Other issues debated are recorded in the Tange Report.

With the disappearance of the Service Departmental Secretaries, it would be necessary to establish the relationship between the Chief of Defence Force Staff and the Secretary of the Defence Department, both housed together and responsible to the Minister. My proposal was

> that the Government distribute elsewhere the powers of the Boards (including the power of administration of the Services and executive command in the case of the Navy), thus permitting abolition of the Boards. This can be done by the Minister for Defence retaining most of the powers and functions given to the Service Boards by statute, regulation or directive; and by delegating some of them through two principal streams, one military and one civilian in the Department of Defence. The powers pertaining to command, discipline and personnel management of the Navy, Army and Air Force should be vested in a Chief of Defence Force Staff and associated senior officers—whether solely or collectively as may be appropriate.

The 'two streams' of administrative control became, when incorporated in legislation in 1975, the so-called 'diarchy' at the centre of the organisation under the Minister. As I shall show, it lived through opposition and misunderstanding, and it administered the newly resurrected 'Defence Force' through several decades that followed. At the time of writing, several modifications have since been made by Coalition Ministers.

My conception of the way the system would work was that practices in the relationship would vary according to the actual content of matters arising for decision or report to the Minister. They could be predominantly military (such as satisfying training or morale concerns); or predominantly financial (such as purchasing or contracting practices). One or the other of the two officers would act, in effect, as *primus inter pares*, by taking the lead in formulating the decision, with the other invited to concur.

Personalities would affect the relationship, as they always had done in past associations among those sharing authority. It would be for Ministers to take this into account when selecting individuals for appointment to the two offices.

I recognised that the obligation on the Secretary to support the Services needed to be confirmed. It would not be sufficient to rely on what new legislation said. Legislation allots authority, but does not specify in what ways it is intended to be used or not used. (This was later confirmed after reading the stark legalese of the 1976 *Defence Reorganisation Act*.) I proposed that the Minister issue directives to the Secretary stating the responsiveness expected of various parts of the Public Service structure to meet the priorities of the Chiefs; and requiring that duty statements reflect the duty. All integrated Service officers would continue to be subject solely to their Chief in respect of discipline. The Chief of Defence Force Staff would have his functions and responsibilities spelled out in regulations.

I now turn to some observations on the general question of civilian–uniform relations in our defence system.

Civilians and Service Officers: Their relative authority

My experiences in earlier years, as already described, indicated to me that the role of civilians would be an issue underlying the response of the Chiefs to my proposals. It is not that attitudes to civilians were identical. The Navy followed the historical Royal Navy tradition of trusting civilians to look after their finances and help in the processes of accountability to Minister and Parliament. The Air Force had few hang-ups about using civilians in subordinate positions on the ground, but subject to an attitude shared with the Navy. That was that civilians should not intrude into specifying what ships, aircraft and weapons systems, and in what numbers, they set out to acquire. I was aware that the Air Force had cause for dissatisfaction with the inability of the civilians in the computer services area of the Department to satisfy their need for reliable records on their enormous inventory of stores.

The Army view of civilians (other than those in subordinate jobs in the commands) was more combative towards civilians in analytical and policy-advising positions—with an expansive view of the role to which Army officers were entitled. Perhaps the explanation for these differences lies in the milieu in which each operated. The possibility of civilians sharing sea-going or flying duties does not arise. The Army administers supplies and personnel in multiple locations throughout Australia and has relations with local authorities.

I recall a good-natured exchange with my colleague (and friend) General A.L. MacDonald, when I observed that the Army seemed to think they could do anything that a civilian does. He replied amiably: 'Yes! And they often do.' This reply omitted to say that each answers to a different authority, one of which is Parliament through the chain of accountability.

The Army's officer corps had the weight of numbers (as many as the other two Services combined); and the advantages of an education system that produced more liberally educated officers at tertiary level than did the other Services, which specialised in engineering and technologies. Indeed there were some officers who left the Army to become prominent scholars. Some Army officers seemed to be less interested in principles of accountability than in the question as to who would exercise the power of decision in any changed arrangements. Historically, the strength of the Defence Department had, over and beyond its once-a-year control of broad expenditure levels and its survey of major equipment proposals, rested on whatever capability it had in reasoned argument. The persuasive strength of this had not easily prevailed against resistance backed by the legislative authority possessed by the Service Boards. Moreover, all Services used unattributed backgrounding of sympathetic journalists to ventilate their chagrin about Defence denials—a technique in public pressure that I was not willing to use myself.

I expected this customary attitude to continue. Entrenched attitudes in institutions are slow to change. Fairhall's injunction 'to think defence' rather than single-Service interests made slow progress in the Army in such matters as accepting credible threat scenarios that foresaw maritime challenges rather than those that justified Army claims for more manpower. This situation was exacerbated, in my view, by the remarkable lack of understanding that I detected in each Service about the needs and problems of the others.

An occasion arose for me to address Army attitudes in a Chief of the General Staff Exercise (under Lieutenant General Sir Mervyn Brogan) in August 1973, as I was heading towards making definite reform proposals. I opened my address as follows: 'What I want to do tonight is to promote some discussion on where you and I fit into the scheme of things.' I went on immediately to refer to the service-civilian relationship, which had fundamental importance and yet, as I said, 'was subject to much prejudice, ignorance and a degree of ribaldry'. There were differences in ethos or credo, in attitude to government, in work-style, and in a willingness to explore the ramifications of complex subjects; 'but the differences are sometimes trivialised and vulgarised by civilians and Servicemen alike'.

I also spoke of the grip on the Services of the experiences of the Second World War, while parliamentary committees went back even further—five and a half decades rather than three as a guide to equipping the Services. In speaking thus,

I also paid respect to the great traditions of the Services that were embedded in our national history.

On a more personal note, addressing the problems that the Department of Defence continued to have, I condemned as a failure of courage that practice of seeking approval from Defence of bids for technology suited to a superpower, leaving it to civilian officials in the Defence Department to propose a more modest and adequate alternative.

The *Bulletin* reported an indignant reaction: 'That would be the most highly offensive address I have listened to, said one General to another.' A well-disposed Major General, who did not share this indignation, later told me that the visiting American Chief of Army had whispered to him: 'This is war.' Whether it would have been more persuasive if it had been less challenging is a matter for judgement. But, as I doubted whether much of what passed between the Secretary and the Chief of the General Staff in our consultations went far into the rest of the officer corps, an audience of so many senior officers had to be made use of to create awareness of changes to come.

Ministerial acceptance of the Recommendations

My consultations drew to a close in late November 1973. With the deadline imminent I was able to report that the several Chiefs 'agreed that the organisation is workable subject to reservations … recorded on certain points' and, in the case of the Chief of Air Staff and Chief of Naval Staff, subject to their reservations being satisfied. We all agreed that experience might call for further changes. I took the lukewarm endorsement by the Chiefs as sufficient to warrant recommending the plan to the Minister. In early December, Barnard met with the Chiefs (and me) to hear any objections they might have. Again the preservation of Service Boards was raised, and I repeated the arguments about inconsistency with the new structure. The Minister gained the approval of the Foreign and Defence Committee of Cabinet, and subsequently of Cabinet itself, with an exception concerning the Department of Supply.

The functions of the Department of Supply, extensive and employing a large staff, had, in Barnard's initiating statement, been left (as I had recommended) for later study and decision. My report recommended that those activities central to defence policy control (such as procurement, contracting of acquisitions and related industry participation and the Scientific Service) be brought into Defence. Management of government factories and other matters I considered optional, though at risk of overloading the Minister if retained. Cabinet decided to put the factories under a separate Minister. I surmised that direction of factories to start producing in areas other than Defence was attractive to a socialist government, and perhaps the unions.

After release of the report, and in the flurry of public criticisms from various directions, it emerged that the Chiefs did not carry all their dispersed regional commanders with them. Some made public protests, the most prevalent being the claim that 'civilians have taken over'. I believe that not only did they not understand the careful distribution of authority that had been drafted, but also the already existing role and authority of the civilians in their own Service Boards. Nor, in some cases, did they understand the established functions of the Defence Department.

Only then did I recognise the limitations of relying on the Service command system to inform subordinates, rather than to issue orders to them. I had wrongly supposed that the careful explanations made during the top-level consultations would be passed down the line. In the event it seemed to me that officers far removed from Canberra, with no previous experience at the policy level in Canberra, were being driven by what they read in the local newspapers and by the rather jaundiced Australian view of public servants (whether state or federal).

The Department was not equipped to engage in a public information programme. Eventually a team of officers from the three Services was sent to explain the intended structure to personnel in the commands around the country. Throughout my term as Secretary I had given addresses at training courses to explain the role required of the Services to conform to the practices of responsible government in a parliamentary democracy, as well as discharge their mission as fighting forces. Given the normal rate of discharges from the Services on age grounds, the impact was probably small. The weakness of understanding of these matters led me earlier to arrange with the then Chief of the General Staff, A. MacDonald, to incorporate some material of this kind in the Army's staff course for its majors. However, the solution required Service leadership from the top.

Members of Parliament and others: Reactions in Parliament and elsewhere—extent of command power

My proposal for the establishment of a number of committees containing representatives of the Services and civilians from the Department came under particular criticism. They were seen as time-wasting ways of frustrating decisions. It was ironic that what I had intended as reassurance that decisions by, for example, an officer of a particular Service, placed in charge of an area of policy, would not be taken without consultation with another Service affected, would be so misrepresented. I had in mind the longstanding rivalry (and occasional outburst of antipathy) between the Air Force and the Navy that I had witnessed in the past. In the event, I decided later that one or two committees were superfluous and did not set them up.

Probably the most extravagant public criticism came from Professor T.B. Millar. Millar was a Duntroon graduate who had retired to academic life with the rank of Lieutenant Colonel. I doubt that he had had experience at the level of Army policy-making and higher administration.

I do not recall any criticisms of my report from my former Minister, Malcolm Fraser. In the Senate, doubts about the intrusion of civilians into command decisions were taken up by the Opposition. Some were concerned about military command being centralised and remote from the battlefield. Much was made of past campaign experience (in which some Senators had been involved 25 years earlier). The Minister did not give the obvious answer that the arrangements left open the delegation of command.

The official definition of command issued by the Chairman of the Chiefs of Staff Committee was as follows:

> Command includes the authority and responsibility for effectively using *available* [my emphasis] resources and for planning the employment of, organising, directing, coordinating and controlling military forces for the accomplishment of assigned duties. It also includes responsibility for the welfare, morale and discipline of personnel under command.

This was read by some as requiring unqualified control of resources needed for military action. One simple fact tended to be overlooked by speakers on both sides of the Parliament and by public commentators on the new organisation. Military command cannot extend to resources that the military do not already have. Yet much of policy activity in Defence, and control by the Defence Department of commitments falling on future budgets, involve requests from the Service Chiefs and not resources in their hands. When the Chiefs express their view of future needs, it comes to Defence in what, in the jargon, is called 'bids'. Examination of the cost-effectiveness, and conformity to other standards in the use of taxpayers' money, is exercised by suitably objective civilian and military officers. This was supposed to be the practice in Service Boards, whose members included a sole civilian who was outweighed by the uniformed petitioners from the various commands. The flaw was the absence of a test of overall Defence effectiveness. This was what the Defence Department, with its limited legal authority, was supposed to remedy.

I did not think it needed to be said that the nearer our commanders got to an actual battlefield, external supervision of their use of resources was bound to be modified. Yet much was made of the view that the recommended organisation was designed for peace and not for war. It was, in my opinion, very unlikely that in 1973 the public and Parliament would agree to a command by the military of money and other resources applicable in a time of war. What was needed was an organisation capable of adaptation, but not necessarily with the immediacy to meet a war without warning. Some doomsayers saw such a war as a possibility in our strategic environment in the 1970s. It was a view that suited the Services wanting more resources. It was not a view shared by me or by those making considered strategic assessments for the Government based on massive sources of information.

Nor did the critics acknowledge the intended use of Ministerial directives to provide safeguards for the Services from a so-called 'civilian takeover'. One such critic who gained media attention was the former Director of Naval Intelligence and then Member of the House of Representatives, later Senator, David Hamer. Writing in the Melbourne *Age* he depicted the Defence Department as having had limited functions in the past and having only recently acquired some increase in authority, leaving the implication that this had been done by the Department's officials. He chose not to acknowledge that Ministers of his own party had recognised the deficiencies in oversight of the Services, and had not shared his disparaging assessment of the professional capabilities of public servants.

Some objectives not achieved

There were other reforms canvassed in my Report which did not come to full fruition. This was partly due to my belief that the civilian side of the Department should not enter into the promotion and appointment practices in respect of the uniformed members of the Services—for reasons of respect for military leadership and for the unique relationship between officers and the rank and file in a fighting Service which were the foundation of morale. The Report suggested areas needing examination by the occupant of the new position of Chief of Defence Force Staff in exercise of his newly acquired power of command. In the event, reforms were few (for reasons that I shall return to later). One example was the failure of the Services, more particularly the two that are oriented to use of complex technology, to fill the posts they were offered in the Defence Department with people possessing, in my judgement, the requisite qualification for the intellectually demanding judgements needed for policy advising. I noted that one Service in particular had a promotion policy that advanced officers with past prowess in combat who could not meet this test. The Air Force had a practice of not promoting to two-star rank officers other than pilots (unless filling the chief engineer's post). The result was the loss, through compulsory age retirement, of men qualified for defence policy advising. The exhortations of Minister Fairhall in the late 1960s were not having the intended results.

Intervention from Defence was needed in other areas in the moulding of a Defence Force out of disparate Services. Establishment practices differed, as did job evaluations, particularly among the many engaged in technical work. Manpower, beyond his control, was a substantial element in the budget that the Secretary of Defence was responsible for preparing.

A Chief of Staff and a civilian administrator look at Service personnel selection, education, training and promotion from different perspectives. The overriding objective is to satisfy the Service Commander's need to have capable leaders of operational activities in war. The civilian adviser to Ministers has the lesser concern of wanting some Service officers to be available with ability to participate in strategic assessments or to assess the cost effectiveness of equipment proposals from Services other than their own; or to judge the risks and advantages of contracting with foreign manufacturers and much else. Such tasks call for analytical capability, fostered by education, as well as proven good judgement and willingness to overlay objective and critical judgement upon their single Service loyalty. The number of positions is small but, because of the unavoidable Service requirement to rotate its personnel, a large number of potential appointees are required throughout the Service at all times.

Streaming of some officers into continuous advising on strategic policy or force structure analysis might not be acceptable, for reasons of morale in which combat leadership rather than desk-bound achievement would command respect. However, I detected no effort to examine this or alternative means of improving the quality of officers available for this area of Service responsibility. It was disturbing to see training courses presented as a substitute for education, and confusion between training (skill in doing things) and education (ability to think). There were also some questionable standards in the free use of the term 'graduate' for some Service courses of study.

I was aware of (and opposed to) the Service demand that each Defence Department posting be rotated among the three Services, irrespective of the quality of people presented for appointment. Value systems for the bringing on of these officers differed from Service to Service. A clue to differences is suggested by noting which Service produced occupants of the top position of Chairman of the Chiefs of Staff Committee and its successor positions in later years. I considered and described the rotation practice as mindless. But ultimately I thought it was for Ministers to direct the Services to raise intellectual standards. In this I was disappointed after Fraser had strongly stated the need for an Australian Defence Academy at tertiary level. Resistance delayed its achievement. Few Ministers after Fairhall and Fraser were interested in this matter. Ministerial objectives can be frustrated by rigid Service practices, or perhaps by poor communication. I recalled Casey, a Minister with great regard for the Services, prevailing upon a Defence Minister in the 1950s to appoint Service Attachés to diplomatic missions in Asia as a way of developing better understanding in the Services of the new environment of Australia's important independent neighbours where they might have to be deployed. I discovered that the Services, far from preserving and spreading the experience of Asia by officers appointed in this way, in most cases sent officers not eligible for promotion and destined to retire from the Service when their two-year posting was finished. I suspected that some appointments were intended as a reward rather than a task (while other officers performed admirably).

Interim arrangements — changes needed in the Department

It was necessary to put aside changes that could only be made when the legislation had been promulgated. But it would have been disastrous to leave matters in limbo for a year, while staff remained uncertain of their future and the disaffected in the regional Service Commands (where most outspoken criticism resided) encouraged the various lobby groups to try to force a re-think on the Government. Accordingly we developed a plan for an interim reorganisation, to be put into effect in chosen areas as soon as staff could be found. While the preparation of my report had imposed a burden on a few (mainly me), the preparation for full integration and reorganisation involved massive changes in legal authorities, preparation of duty statements, directives, documentation setting out chains of financial control and much else. The burden on civilian and military staff in the Department during 1973 was substantial. All of this was superimposed on the normal daily activities of the Department (budgetary and otherwise), as well as various requirements arising from our international associations described elsewhere in this memoir.

Until such time as the new command arrangements became law, the Services continued to be governed by their Boards and, the positions of Departmental Secretaries having been abolished by an impetuous government decision (referred to elsewhere), I had to accept their former responsibility. For practical reasons, I obtained approval to have the three individuals appointed as special deputies to act as my agents on the respective Boards.

Once the new Act was promulgated, each of the Services had to review and change its command structure. It was necessary for each Chief, now in sole command and made entirely responsible for what went on in his Service, to have the backing of specialist advisers, revised lines of command and, perhaps most importantly, effective arrangements for coordination and cooperation. For example, the Air Force, because of its highly advanced technology and given the vulnerability of air safety as well as combat readiness to any shortcomings in the association of engineering maintenance with the supply function and its vast inventory, had some perplexing problems to address. In the Air Force and in the other Services, time had to be allowed for careful review by suitable teams during 1975. The absence of any immediate threat made it possible to proceed slowly.

While awaiting the passage of the reorganisation legislation, I went ahead with changes not dependent on legislation. There were also changes in the top military staff due to retirements. Admiral Sir Victor Smith retired after five years as Chairman of the Chiefs of Staff Committee, being replaced by General Sir

Francis Hassett (who became the first Chief of Defence Force Staff in 1976). He was followed by General Sir Arthur MacDonald, and he in turn by Admiral Sir Anthony Synnot (who was my co-administrator when I severed my connection with Defence in August 1979).

I made changes in the civilian staff. An early objective was to get effective control of the tasking and priorities of the Defence scientific and technical laboratories. This purpose was assisted by the energy of Farrands as Chief Defence Scientist, who also contributed more than his predecessor (Wills) to defence policy decisions.

Much of their work was of the highest quality in the opinion of the American and British with whom they shared much advanced and innovative research. Yet some parts of the system had grown up primarily serving the production and repair activities of defence factories when all were part of the Supply Department. They tended to act for the Services as problem-solvers, and the connection with the policy objectives of the Department of Defence was tenuous. The appointment of a Chief Defence Scientist in the Department had been one of the half-baked reforms of 1958. Without any control over the laboratories dispersed around Australia or any organic link with the fast-moving technologies and new research findings, the occupant of the post in Canberra had become a rather detached science guru, expected to offer off-the-cuff opinions on weapons acquisitions and maintenance problems. Under my changes he was given new line authority, through appropriate procedures; and in later years there were more radical changes to the management of this important part of our national defence capabilities.

I also drew some of the scientists into becoming analysts in Canberra in the enhanced role of systems analysis of Service bids for new weapons systems and platforms.

Managing the Department—The 1973 political environment

I now return to the early days of the new Labor Administration. There were many unexpected problems to deal with while simultaneously developing the reorganisation.

For example, a January 1973 publication of some classified information roused interest in the attitude of Ministers towards security in the context of its belief in open government. A classified minute of the Defence Committee appeared in the media. In some sensitive areas public servants were feeling concern about the willingness (or ability) of Ministers to control the activities of private office advisers who were enthusiastically taking it upon themselves to implement open-government policies. Barnard's staff, consisting of Clem Lloyd, a long-time adviser during his Opposition years, and Brian Toohey, a self-assured journalist, exhibited distrust of the Department's loyalty to Labor's mandate—or perhaps its understanding of it, particularly in respect of matters under attack by the Labor Left, of which the American defence connection was a prime example. There was a related problem. For the first time in my experience, a Department could not be sure that submissions and reports sent to the Minister actually reached his desk. When, as I shall relate, both of these appointees departed, I was told of papers having been sidetracked in this way.

There was a certain irony in this, given the propensity of those suspicious of the Public Service to accuse us of withholding information in order to serve some agenda or policy bias of our own, a charge which in my case at least was as baseless as the alternative, which was that we set out to confuse Ministers by 'snowing' them with a surfeit of paper. The Labor movement is notorious for inventing conspiracies perhaps because, as I have heard its critics say, it sometimes organises them against its own.

We were entering an era when people with ideological convictions, but with no experience of the problems and constraints that fall on Ministers of any party when they enter Cabinet, were setting up as rivals to seasoned departmental advisers. Later administrations learned to make room for both sources of advice. It was beneficial for career public servants to be relieved of such tasks as preparing material for Ministers to discredit political opponents. But no precepts were laid down: Whitlam was content simply to issue a minatory direction to Departmental Secretaries not to issue instructions to Ministerial Staff. What was needed was a policy *modus vivendi*. Fortunately in our case, Barnard's later staff replacements established harmonious relations with his Department.

Disclosure of the American presence—Conflict with Labor Left

In the early days there was pressure on Barnard from two directions on the subject of American activities on Australian soil. There were demands for disclosure of the nature of certain installations while, on the other hand, the Americans wanted reassurance that defence activities important to them conducted in cooperation with Australia would not be nullified by disclosures from which the Soviet Union in particular would be the beneficiary.

After examination, it was shown that not all American activities required secrecy and Barnard was able to describe them to Parliament. Two installations were in a different category.[1] They had the highest significance in the nuclear standoff between the United States and the Soviet Union. They were the Joint Defence Space Research Facility at Pine Gap near Alice Springs, and the Joint Defence Space Communications Facility at Nurrungar near Woomera in the North of South Australia (near the site where earlier British ballistic missile experiments had been conducted).

Physical isolation from hostile intercepts, and from monitoring of the downlinks to the satellite dishes that later became a prominent part of the landscape, along with an available airfield and housing, were considerations which led the original exploring parties to recommend these sites. For the Americans, the trustworthiness of its Australian ally was doubtless vital in their final decision to select Australia.

Whitlam's and Barnard's conflict in Parliament with the Left, and with the Party at large, deepened in January and February 1973 over the Government's modification of its pledged withdrawal of all Army units from Asia. Publication of an explanation, which breached security, of a secret intelligence activity added a problem of a different kind. Having been told that the ground forces in Singapore contained an unacknowledged signals intelligence unit for which there was no immediate alternative site, the Ministers decided to retain 600 troops there. The decision and the reason found their way into the media without acknowledgment of the source. The Leader of the Opposition (Billy Snedden) surmised that the Prime Minister had given an off-the-record briefing. Whatever the source, there was an added reason for Australia's intelligence partners to be concerned as they watched for signs in the new Government of a slackening of protection of the information they entrusted to Australia. That extended beyond classified intelligence to weaponry, operational techniques and much else. Calming their anxieties—usually but not always unfounded—was to occupy me at various times during the Labor regime.

The Department had now to help the Minister contend with further troubles within the Labor Party over the American defence connection in general, but directed particularly at the Government's announced refusal to disclose what went on in the Joint Facilities at Pine Gap and Nurrungar. My own attention to these serious policy matters became complicated in late February and early March by a distracting political storm over an inherently less important matter—the alleged treatment by me of Barnard's office staff—to which I shall return later.

Suspicion had built up in the Labor Party while in Opposition, as it had in various public interest groups, over these facilities about which Labor leaders had been denied any information to justify the secrecy covering them. Labor Ministers were able to point to the contrasting treatment of the Coalition leader when in Opposition. In my External Affairs days in the 1950s, the then Government rejected suggestions from time to time that Labor's then leader (Evatt) be 'briefed'. The idea of an Australian equivalent of Britain's Privy Councillor's oath to respect confidentiality on matters of state had been canvassed but not proceeded with. Ironically, such a briefing offered on one occasion was turned down by Labor itself as potentially muzzling them from opposing policies that deserved to be attacked.

There were troubles, too, within the Labor Ministry when, following discussion with Departments, the Whitlam/Barnard leadership adopted the longstanding practice of confining access to certain high security matters to Ministers who had a demonstrable 'need-to-know' relevant to their portfolio. The demand for equality among Ministers put this in contention by those left out. In December, at a meeting called by the Prime Minister, I witnessed an invasion by several Ministers not invited because the defence subjects for discussion lay outside their portfolio responsibilities.

Newly appointed members of a Ministry that had never had the responsibility of preserving the confidences of allies, or of knowing what their content was, would understandably resent being kept in the dark while others (including officials) were not. They were touchy too. Barnard told me that there had been a reaction from some Ministers when they saw that a submission of mine had innocently suggested that a certain question 'would be for future governments to decide'. 'Predicting—maybe even plotting our downfall!'

A decision on the Government's intentions towards public disclosure on security matters came to a head when the two leaders addressed the demands for release of information about what came to be called 'American bases' and, from some quarters, their expulsion from Australia.

The Joint US–Australian Defence Facilities

One of my first actions after the 1972 election had been to arrange for the Prime Minister and Minister to be informed of the nature, purpose, and capability of the activities at Pine Gap and Nurrungar. For the purpose of this memoir I can find authority, and the degree of detail permissible by way of explanation, in official announcements made by the then Prime Minister, Bob Hawke, and the Minister for Defence, Kim Beazley, in the 1980s.

As recorded earlier, the Chief Defence Scientist, Dr John Farrands, and I were privy to the operations. In addition, each of us had paid visits to the sites at various times and had been given demonstrations of their capabilities and of the type of data collected. I had been given assurances at the site that activities in Australia were not made targets for information gathering and had heard this reinforced when accompanying Ministers in high-level meetings in Washington.

The Hawke statements in 1989 declared that 'among the functions performed are the provision of early warning by receiving from space satellites information about missile launches and the provision of information about the occurrence of nuclear explosions'. The statements went on to refer to the existence of 'other technical functions', disclosure of which would damage both American and Australian interests. In October of that year Defence Minister Beazley enlarged on the advantages of the data derived. Hawke had stressed, and Beazley now repeated, the contribution made to achieving current and prospective nuclear force reductions by the assured verification that agreements on this, and bans on nuclear testing, were being honoured. Without such verification, no American commitment to force reduction would get through Congress.

Beazley declared in addition that the Facilities contributed most significantly to the avoidance of a catastrophic war (something in my opinion even more fundamental than preserving promises to disarm). By way of explanation, Beazley pointed out that there was danger in either side miscalculating the other's intentions and getting in first by initiating a nuclear attack. Because of that, 'early warning systems take the guesswork out of the situation and greatly diminish the interest that either side could possible have in initiating nuclear war'. Warning of a launch (along with other means of tracking the location of impact) would give time for a retaliatory launch against the attacker.

Later statements specified the different roles of Pine Gap and Nurrungar while nevertheless declining to publish details of operations and methods.

Fifteen years earlier we were not in a position to claim the existence of all these advantages when advising our Ministers. To be certain that possession of the early warning capability would deter a first strike rested on the assumption that the knowledge had been convincingly conveyed to the Russians; and Australia was not a party to the dialogue between the two superpowers. Moreover, Leonid Brezhnev's Soviet Union was exerting unrelenting pressure both in political propaganda in Europe and in nuclear deployments at that time. Arms control agreements were not in place. Some arguments justifying the Facilities, of a kind that would mollify if not satisfy opposition in the Labor Movement, were therefore not available to Whitlam and Barnard. As to the value for deterrence of the Soviet Union, we officials had no independent evidence that the early warning capability had been conveyed to them. In effect, we had to accept American assurances to us of the vital importance of the data, without any comprehensive understanding as to what effect it was being used. In my advising, I accepted that the United States would not itself initiate a first nuclear strike—a view not universally shared within the Labor Party.

Our knowledge of the data being collected satisfied me that it would be used by the United States to maintain its military capability of matching the Soviet Union's advances. I saw the preservation of this capability (what in the later Hawke years was described as 'strategic stability') as the principal benefit to the security of Western democracies.

There was another dimension—ANZUS, under which the Facilities agreement with the Americans had, in its terms, been declared to rest. No alternative sites could be said to be available. I believed that unilateral steps to terminate the agreements would have profound consequences for the American interpretation of what we were entitled to expect from them under the ANZUS Treaty, and for our standing as an ally; and that this in turn would alter the perception in [the region to our north][2] of the strength with which Australia could be defended.

In the briefing of Ministers, I do not recall any necessity to labour these points.

As regards my own convictions as an adviser, then and later, I should add that the value to Australia, beyond the contribution that we were making to the nuclear balance, was far reaching. Our scientists learned for the first time of techniques of using space phenomena to study terrestrial objects in detail. To apply the data to practical applications in our own decision-making was more difficult, because the Americans in contrast had a vast machine in which to correlate the input from the Facilities with other sources that they possessed. We believed we were told all that we needed to know. There was a valuable inflow of highly sensitive material to our system not confined to this subject.

A complete balance sheet of the benefits gained by Australia by allowing Australian sovereign territory to be used in this way would require us to look beyond Pine Gap and Nurrungar. It would require bringing to account the strong flow of information received on a preferential basis about American tests of weapons systems, sensors and their software used in our own equipment decisions, and for which there was no substitute at that high level of technology.

Beyond assessing the value to us of the ANZUS alliance lay the great policy question as to how far Australia was ready to make this contribution to the global security of the Western democracies while the Soviet threat was unabated and, in some respects, becoming greater with the deployment of new nuclear missiles targeted against Europe. It was this contribution which some of the protesters breaking down the fences at Pine Gap were wanting to halt.

In reporting all that we knew to the Ministers in private briefings, we were in a position to enlarge considerably on the matters which, as I have said, Hawke was later to describe enigmatically in public as 'other technical functions'.

The Ministers decided to accept the continued presence of the Facilities, subject to the Americans agreeing to greater participation and observation by Australian personnel, and to recommend this course to the Labor Party.

They remained shackled by the limited amount of information they could disclose in order to satisfy party and public. As administrator of a policy of such national importance, my task was easier. Primarily, it was to preserve secrecy and to reassure our allies on the point. Over and above guarding against wilful breaches of security, my experience told me of the necessity to prevent leakages of secrets from carelessness or from people with an urge to parade their unique possession of information. Potential risks of this kind had increased with the influx to positions of trust of people openly scornful of the security practices thought to belong to outdated Coalition party attitudes towards informing the public.

Keeping secrets requires some drastic practical measures which attract criticism and no doubt accusations of excessive zeal. I took a highly restrictive view of those entitled to know the unpublished functions of the Facilities. If Ministers had to be informed of developments in writing, I conveyed it personally by hand, declining to use the customary procedure of trusting Ministerial staff to place material before a Minister.

My objective was not secrecy for its own sake. It was to prevent the Soviet Union learning about a vital intelligence activity by reading the newspapers simultaneously with the Australian public. Within the Government there had been a strictly limited 'listing' procedure. Most of the Public Service was excluded, including members of my own Department and Foreign Affairs except at the very top. I kept personal control of any discussions with the Americans that developments might make necessary. Barnard approved the list and the procedure I was following when he was preparing his statement to be made to Parliament on 28 February 1973.

There was a concurrent need to get Ministerial acceptance of the practice of resisting media probing into defence secrets by cumulative speculative gambits. Whitlam readily agreed, and announced, that it would be settled policy 'neither to confirm nor deny' speculations about defence secrets.

Apart from damage to our interests that might follow unauthorised revelations on matters in which the Americans (or the British) were concerned, I formed the impression that it was a matter of honour for Whitlam to ensure that arrangements legally made under undertakings of confidentiality were implemented. Equally I thought there was a touch of naïveté in his respect of the sovereign rights of the Republic of Singapore when he terminated an Australian intelligence unit operating out of that base.

The Americans took precautions to avoid speculation when any senior official in their intelligence community visited the Facilities. On the other hand, it was possible to be open about the visits of defence officials. I myself accompanied the then Deputy Secretary for Defense, David Packard, on such a visit when he demonstrated in this way the strategic importance to the United States of the Pine Gap Facility.

Australia could claim to have been highly successful in maintaining secrecy in those years. Later some speculations by academics eroded the secrecy.

Limited disclosure on Pine Gap and Nurrungar

For the Ministers, the pressure from the Labor Party, the media and interest groups for more information remained. In the Department we found it difficult to find new suggestions to offer, given the constraints. The best I could suggest, without injury to the truth, was for the Government to declare that 'neither station is part of a weapons system and neither station can be used to attack any country'. This formula was used by Barnard in the February statement to Parliament. (Beazley's statement 16 years later was not very different, although he was then free to add much more).[3]

In his statement Barnard listed all the installations in which US activities were conducted. He described the functions of several installations that were contributing to the monitoring of conformity to the Test Ban Treaty.

As to the Pine Gap/Nurrungar twins he said that, in the light of what Labor now knew, they would want to make some changes; but they were governed by treaties that gave them current tenure. We would protect them from unauthorised disclosure; and he declared that, more widely, Labor would protect all classified information entrusted to us by the United States, Britain and others. He certified that 'the details of the techniques employed, and of the data being tested and analysed at the two stations must be kept highly secret if the two stations are to continue to serve their objectives'.

He went on to offer a political palliative. Members of Parliament must have a special right of access to the two installations, which will enable them 'to see something of the nature of the operations'—all subject to orderly procedures. In passing, he said that 'only the very few people directly associated with the central execution of the defence programmes of the United States and Australia' would have greater access to information.

His words confirmed publicly that the limitation that I had exercised on dissemination of information in the Departments and Services would continue under Ministerial authority.

There ensued a visit to me by a team of American officials, led by Ambassador Walter Rice, expressing concern about the consequences for security of disclosure of further details about the operations of the Facilities. They complained about the intention to allow visits by Australian Parliamentarians when there was uncertainty as to what seeing 'something of the nature of the operations' would mean in practice. I had the Minister's authority to tell the Americans that access would not be unlimited and that their secrets would be protected. I was not able to predict how little interest our politicians later showed in visiting the sites. But I had to speak bluntly to the visitors following some remarks to me about the erosion of American rights and the lack of an equivalent right of American Congressmen to pay such visits. I said that 'they would be a long way from their electorate whereas some of our members of Parliament would not be'. Our Parliament had to be satisfied for its part that Australian sovereignty was being respected.

I have observed that American engineers responsible for the brilliant technologies of the stations working in outer space, like those in the US Navy on occasions, were not always sensitive to the political facts of life in sovereign states. Moreover, confidentiality about the Facilities was sometimes eroded by leakages to journals in America, probably as a result of much of the research and production of equipment being contracted out to private industries.

When Caucus was shown the intended statement, there was, according to press reports (including one by Toohey, Barnard's lately departed Private Secretary), a storm of criticism and a heavy vote of opposition which delayed presentation to Parliament. It was reported that only the strongest intervention by the Prime Minister saved Barnard from having the plan repudiated. A prompt offer by the Americans to discuss changes helped, I was told, to placate the Party critics.

Labor's problem with the North West Cape Naval Communications Station

Review of some of the other arrangements with the Americans remained unfinished business in 1974. The United States Naval Communications Station was controlled and manned exclusively by Americans. They enjoyed some privileges, although not as many as those they had sought when negotiating with Sir Garfield Barwick (the then Minister for External Affairs) in 1963 to establish the radio relay station with a very low frequency capacity to communicate with submerged submarines. Then Barwick gave the Americans an authoritative (and cheerfully didactic) lesson on the Federal Constitution and on State jurisdiction. When the US Navy spokesman plaintively explained his need to avoid giving the Portuguese a precedent for an agreement limiting American rights in their territory, Barwick had bluntly said: 'Brother! This is not Portugal.'

I confess to having in later years no great understanding of Labor's objections. None of the rights given to the Americans seemed to prejudice Australian security; moreover, the Station enabled us to communicate with our own submarines in the sea depths. American declared policy renounced any intention to launch a first nuclear strike and the Labor objection seemed to me to have much to do with symbols, and with their objection in 1973 to the provision that the agreement 'did not carry with it any degree of control of the Station or of its use'. Labor, when in opposition at the time, had declared this to be an infringement of Australian sovereignty. More substantial was the question of whether we were offering the Soviet Union a nuclear target. This issue, whether a probability or not, would remain an indeterminate question of high policy at the political level (Beazley offered an answer in the 1980s). Barnard was able to obtain agreement to have more Australians working in the Station. The Americans held out, reasonably in my opinion, against Australians being privy to the contents of their coded commands (the practical value of which was uncertain since not all commands would pass though this Station in a threatening situation because of deliberate redundancy in the American control system which had multiple channels).

While Barnard was in office, some changes were made giving Australians a greater role. In later years, when Labor was in Opposition, arguments revived about the possibility of the Station being the channel for American strategic commands to direct military action for objectives that Australia did not approve. Bill Hayden referred to fears of a shift in American naval strategy, from preserving stable deterrence of the Soviet Union to the adoption of a warfighting role for its nuclear force, in which Australia would have no say in the use of our territory for relaying commands which might have cataclysmic consequences. This argument was resisted by the Fraser Government when in power; yet the most convincing rejection came from Labor itself in the 1980s. Labor's Kim Beazley then pointed out that any such major shift in American strategy would require, as a prelude, a far-reaching restructuring of that country's capabilities, open to be observed by us and everybody else. He and the Hawke Government strongly endorsed Australia's contributing to a stable superpower balance. Beazley said:

> The Naval Communications Station at North West Cape supports the most invulnerable leg of the triad, the submarine-based missile force. These weapons are the final guarantor of deterrence. Any threat to the vital communications links to these submarines would undermine the security and effectiveness of the submarine-launched missiles they carry.[4]

Hayden's warped dissatisfaction with the Station led him into an attack on me personally that seemed to be the product of his misunderstanding of its basic purpose. Prime Minister Fraser having approved the briefing of the Leader of the Opposition, I had been instructed to inform him of all sensitive and secret activities involving intelligence gathering. This I did comprehensively in the Department's office. Later, Hayden complained to Killen that I had failed to inform him about North West Cape (which was not an intelligence operation). His letter became public and appeared to make a case of untrustworthiness on my part. I was incensed at yet another slur on my integrity, this time under parliamentary privilege. I told Killen that I did not think that my duty extended to conducting such briefings again unless the Minister was present to certify in Parliament, if necessary, that I had not been misleading. I was not sure that I ever got a response from Killen—which is one way of disposing of a nuisance.

The Lloyd affair—Barnard's rebuke of Tange

The British Government's new Defence Secretary, Lord Carrington, included Australia in a tour of Southeast Asia. I felt that his visit in early 1973 would not be entirely welcome so early in the life of our Government, and might rouse fears of 'heavying' by a major defence power. But Carrington was received cordially by Ministers. His purpose was to ascertain whether Australia would continue to hold to its commitments under the Five Power Defence Arrangements with Malaysia and Singapore alongside Britain, entered into by the Whitlam Government's predecessors. Uncertainty had been created by the announced withdrawal of Army units. Britain's intentions would be affected by those of Australia. After the consultation with Barnard, and their frank discussion of the outlook, Carrington publicly declared himself to be well satisfied.

For my part, I had renewed a longstanding friendship which went back to 1956 when Carrington was appointed British High Commissioner to Australia. His young family and mine shared outings and picnics in Canberra, and we kept in touch afterwards. More recently he had stayed several days with me in the Australian residence in New Delhi, in preference to the British residence (and demonstrated his duck-shooting prowess in lakes in the Punjab). But his visit had some less pleasant consequences for me.

Lloyd alleged that my administrative arrangements for the conference with Carrington prompted his resignation from Barnard's office and, with the help of sympathetic friends in the press and in the Labor movement, he stimulated a sustained attack on Barnard. The focus was on Barnard's supposed inability to control his Departmental Secretary and on my allegedly exceeding my duty. That blended well with the conviction in Labor Party Left circles, particularly the Victorian Left, who alleged that I was a kind of Menzies relic, subservient to American defence interests and incapable of supporting Labor's platform.

In fact, what was to blame was confusion in communication and, on Barnard's part, an extraordinary (and, to me, inexplicable) lack of contact between Barnard and his employee, who was sitting outside his office when he was in Canberra.

The sequence of events had been that Lloyd (without, I was told, seeking any authority from his boss) applied to my staff to be included in the group of advisers to sit behind Barnard in the talks with Carrington. When I learned of this, Barnard was in Launceston, where he remained for several days, contactable only by telephone. I spoke to him, saying that I thought it unusual to include a Private Secretary; and that this one did not carry the security clearance needed in the event that certain joint intelligence arrangements came under discussion. After saying that he had had in mind someone other than Lloyd, Barnard agreed to drop the idea of either attending. In consequence I told my staff to tell Lloyd he would not be included. Thereafter, both the Minister and the orchestrated critics in Canberra took offence at my giving a direction to one of his personal staff. Barnard later changed his mind and one of his staff did attend. To avoid public argument with my Minister, I wrote a minute recording my view of events. I began by including the pointed words, 'you decided the composition of the group of advisers to attend the Ministerial Defence Conference'. To assist him to justify publicly his own misunderstanding of the course of events, I included the word 'apologise'. Neither then, nor as I record the events now, did I believe that I had anything to apologise about.

But the storm blew right out of the teacup when the Opposition (with no thanks from me for their helpfulness) initiated several days of questions about the ill-treatment not of Lloyd but of Tange. They lent on the remark by Barnard that he had 'reservations' about my report that he had tabled in the House. It was a new experience for me to be the subject of multi-column headlines in the major dailies. I accepted the judgement of the shrewd Alan Reid that I was not the important target, but a scapegoat in the continued campaign against the Barnard/Whitlam leadership and their softer line on defence cooperation with the United States.[5]

As the *Canberra Times* observed on 8 March 1973: 'Sir Arthur has to put up with the occupational hazard of being the silent partner in a difference with his Ministerial superior.' In fact I remained silent and refused all the many media requests for an interview.

On 8 March the Deputy Leader of the Opposition, Doug Anthony, had, I have no doubt, my interest in mind along with an obvious political motivation, in calling on the Prime Minister to speak to me to ascertain the facts and to clear the name of (as he said) 'one of Australia's most experienced and highly regarded public servants'. But more reassuring for me, as I needed the trust of the Government so that I could get on with so much unfinished business, was to read that the Prime Minister, in confirming in his statement in the House his total confidence in his Defence Minister, also foresaw his Minister putting to use the talents he attributed to me. That evening, Barnard told a (possibly disappointed) television journalist that he did not want a new Permanent Head.

I addressed a minute to Barnard saying plainly that, after so many days without a face-to-face discussion, I would like one now. He then confided to me some details of difficulties of his own during his association with Lloyd—a confidence that I have no intention of breaching. It seems probable to me that Lloyd, a man of some intellectual substance, had some difficulty, emotional and otherwise, in translating from the calm of an adviser to a political leader in Opposition with no responsibility for national affairs, to a position requiring some response to the high national policy issues for decision swirling past him to his employer's desk. He later joined the staff of a University where I understand he gained respect for the quality of his research and writings.[6]

Redefining the threat basis for Defence planning

During my years as a member of the Defence Committee, I had observed how much ambiguity lay in the single word 'threat'. Some (in Parliament and in the

Services) would see a 'threat to Australia' in a military build-up or threatening posture to neighbours by a Communist power distant from Australia. Others looked for evidence nearer to the territories and seas in the approaches to Australia. A consequence of this confusion appeared in concrete form in sharp differences in the debates with the Services about the strategic relevance of the weapons systems and weapons platforms they sought approval to procure.

Historically, under the Menzies and succeeding conservative governments, the idea had lingered on that any shot fired in anger around the world was a potential threat to Australia—not necessarily to Australian territory but to 'Australia'. This view had its origins in our earlier acceptance of collective security and commitment to Imperial defence planning and action. A corollary of this belief, which had profound effects on how we spent our defence budgets, was that threats could arise without warning. It was a belief deeply embedded in the Services, where it provided a rationale for their training and their claim for only the latest technology.

As already indicated, we addressed this subject in the 1972 Defence Review. Early in the 1970s analysts in the Joint Intelligence Organisation, headed by Robert Furlonger and his successor in 1973 Gordon Jockel, were exploring another aspect of threats—their imminence. This entailed whether making assumptions about what the strategic situation would be in the 1980s was justified. Because of the hazards of predicting the future, 'futurology' was scorned by many as vaporous speculation, providing no sound basis for protecting the country. Yet the fact was that calculations of the future were implicit in every decision made by Cabinets and Service Chiefs and in all policy advice about the procurement of long-living capital assets, and even in the direction of training which, if strategic requirements changed unexpectedly, could only be redirected with time. Australian practice kept ships in service for 25 and even 30 years; and aircraft almost as long. While the systems they carried could be modified if international events called for it, past decisions heavily committed the future. Moreover, you cannot easily change the location or capabilities of static bases like an airfield, naval repair facilities or even Army training bases. They rested on past assumptions about where threats would need to be countered.

As Barnard prepared for his first budget in 1973, he asked for a review of Australia's strategic prospects and of the probability of threats to Australia occurring. At the time there was confidence that nuclear deterrence was effective.

Labor had made clear its intention to focus Defence objectives on the defence of Australian territory (without necessarily renouncing deployments outside Australia serving that purpose). It followed that a strategic review should not be devoted to analysing outbreaks of violence or a build-up of forces in locations remote from Australia, or involving the balance between the superpowers where Australia's military capabilities would not be significant. Indiscriminate findings of 'threats' needed to be curbed. Drawing on analysis by the Joint Intelligence Organisation under Jockel, we persuaded the Defence Committee to present a threat assessment which addressed more specifically than before the time it would take for development of a threat of a kind and intensity to require a significant Australian military response. This judgement should be the foundation for many current decisions on such matters as stockpiles, factory capacity and the timing of weapon repair or acquisitions.

Malaysia and Singapore had developed strength and confidence was growing. The assessment found no immediate threat to the territory of Australia. It foresaw that this situation would be likely to remain for 10 years, extending even to 15 years, while recognising that there had to be uncertainty about those final years. The Report acknowledged that this uncertainty left a problem in making decisions in some elements of the force structure, because the acquisition of some equipments (and personnel skills to operate them) had a particularly long lead-time.

It was a bold new assessment in the face of past findings of threats worldwide. When Barnard announced his acceptance of it, there was an outburst of criticism, and some derision. Some academics (Professor Tom Millar being one) attacked the predictions. Some sought to refute the finding by measuring the lapse of time between the end of war somewhere and the outbreak of another somewhere else, producing what I thought to be a worthless and irrelevant contribution to deciding what we needed for this continent located in the Southwest Pacific and our nearer Asian environment. Faith in Australia's subjection to the 'peace is indivisible' notion of global involvement was still with us.

A concept growing out of the revised threat assessment was that there would be adequate warning time to prepare, provided we made full use of all the intelligence and surveillance resources, and of Foreign Affairs advice and that of allies. 'Warning time' lasted many years as a doctrinal basis for testing proposals for equipment and personnel growth. In later years, I understand it was displaced by recognition that some small-scale but testing threats to our territory or to other external interests could come with little warning. This led to a major shift of military units northwards and in other ways.

Under the revised threat estimate, some reductions were made in Barnard's time in defence industry production and in the holding of stocks. But, in respect of major defence equipments, some questionable replacement decisions won the day. For my part I later felt I should have opposed the replacement of the aged *Centurion* tank, given the difficulty of foreseeing a theatre requiring its deployment. It is not only politicians who are cautious about surrendering an area of unique expertise and training: the aircraft carrier was to be a later *cause célèbre*. As regards the tank, senior Departmental analysts were influenced by the seriousness of what would be an irretrievable decision to terminate the Army's possession of this special operational expertise.

The Department's analysts had difficulty in finding a basis upon which to assess the Navy's claim to replace its light destroyer fleet progressively with the same numbers, but with enhanced modern firepower and surveillance capabilities. The generalities of the Strategic Guidance paper, set beside a government policy of concentrating on defence closer to home, were little help in assessing the need for capabilities to operate in far distant waters. The decision to replace the light destroyer project with the American-developed patrol frigate was a decision based not on strategy but on the risk that the complexities of marrying advanced sensors, firepower and hull design without unacceptable delays might be beyond Australia's capabilities.

Barnard in Opposition in 1972 had criticised the continuing growth during the planning in the size of what had set out to be a light destroyer. He had called for a new programme of patrol boats for coastal protection.

The problem of deriving a statement of military requirements from the generalisations of the Strategic Guidance document remained throughout the Barnard–Morrison period, and continued under Killen when the Fraser Ministry came to power.[7]

All the Chiefs complained that the Department gave them only the somewhat abstract findings of the periodic 'Strategic Basis' document, drafted by Defence and Foreign Affairs officials and endorsed by the Chiefs in the Defence Committee, as their Bible.

It was certainly not as precise as the Ten Commandments. I could see the Chief's problem, but I believed that it was beyond the experience and the responsibility of public servants under my leadership to propose what formations and equipment, in what locations, the Army should have; or whether the divisional structure should be retained; or the most suitable locations for the assets of the Air Force; or which ports justified countermine measures or new berthing facilities; or at a more general level, the preferred emphasis as between air to surface capabilities, as against air superiority or sub-surface means.

This area was, in my opinion, one for action by the Chief of Defence Force Staff. But it was largely unoccupied territory up to the time of my retirement and, as I understand it, remained so until the 1980s. Then, under a perceptive Defence Minister, Kim Beazley, a civilian public servant was charged with the task. Dr Paul Dibb brought to bear his accumulated experience of dealing with all three Services, his grasp of strategy and his experience in intelligence assessments. In addition, he had a much needed persuasive personality. The Dibb Report of March 1986 was accepted broadly by the Hawke Government.

Barnard's negotiations with Washington

Towards the end of 1973 Barnard made an extensive overseas tour. He included Washington, a visit to which is essential for any Defence Minister. In his case it was to set down some anxieties and negotiate some changes in certain agreements.

Before the visits in January 1974 for discussion with US Defense Secretary James Schlesinger and the Pentagon, Barnard had already arranged some changes, readily conceded, with the newly arrived Ambassador, Marshall Green. Green was a unique appointment—the most senior career man to occupy the Embassy, having been an Assistant Secretary in the Department of State. Some close to him let it be known that the more important post of Japan would have been his preference. Previous American Ambassadors had owed their appointment to favours to the political party of the President—usually money but in the case of William Battle in the 1950s, friendship with John Kennedy. Battle had been one of the few exceptions to a line of unrelieved mediocrity in occupancy of the post. Green was certainly not in that category, but his appointment was no compliment to Australia. Green was sent because of apprehension about Whitlam's policies and Nixon's resentment at the statements of some of his wilder Ministers.

In the event, I doubt that much calming influence on Washington was needed from Green once Whitlam made his intentions clearer. Indeed one high-ranking American told me that Green was given to sending somewhat alarmist reports to Washington. This of course is a fairly normal practice of competent trouble-shooters who are disappointed by the meagre trouble upon which to apply their skill. Nevertheless, when the man to take over as Acting Prime Minister during Whitlam's frequent absences abroad, Dr Cairns, became the new Deputy Leader elected by Caucus, one can assume some heightened concern based on his earlier statements on American policies.

Barnard was received in Washington with a cordiality that probably owed something to his status as Deputy Prime Minister. I did harbour a cynical suspicion that the Americans were out to impress (just as in earlier days we had seen lavish and generous British hospitality as a form of 'duchessing' of Australian Ministers). The Americans in official talks are business-like and not given to time wasting. Their day starts early and ends late; and the superpower has a stream of official visitors. But their entertainment in elegant historic venues is stylish and generous (but with a bias towards fruit juice as a beverage). US Secretary of State Dr Henry Kissinger attended a reception for Barnard, which I was told he rarely did for such visitors.

Following the preliminary work with Green in Australia, Barnard and Schlesinger agreed on changes wanted by Barnard in the North West Cape agreement, limiting the land occupied and appointing an Australian Deputy Commander.

There was a good airing of views on the international security situation, and clarification of one Australian action that worried the Americans. Australia had suspended visits to some ports by American nuclear-powered warships. (Whether they carried nuclear weapons was a separate matter and in any case not for discussion, because of the American policy of declining for security reasons to confirm or deny the presence of such weapons in any particular location.)

The suspension was intended to last until Australian scientists had surveyed the ports to ascertain what berths (or what ports) occupied by such ships contained a risk to vulnerable populations (or institutions such as hospitals) in the event of an accident (such as collision) that released irradiated matter, such as steam, into the atmosphere. We were not fobbed off by the US Navy, present at the talks, continuing to tell us disingenuously that they berthed their vessels without hesitation on the Hudson River alongside Manhattan Island. The characteristics of wind direction and some other factors were unique to each location and each needed to be assessed as a prerequisite to giving a safety all clear. The chances of accident were remote but the assessment had to be made and reported to Parliament.

Barnard explained all this, but I thought I detected some scepticism in Schlesinger (who had formerly been in charge of American nuclear energy programmes). I took him aside privately to assure him that Australia's new Labor Government was not in this matter moved by some obscurantist fear of nuclear power generation as such, or confusion with nuclear weaponry. We had a Parliament to be satisfied by Australian rather than American scientists. This was a political reality in Australia. While Schlesinger said teasingly that he suspected there was a bit of obscurantism at work, he did not pursue the American objection to our suspension of visits.

But not so the US Navy—or at least part of it. Approaching the lunch table I was accosted by the formidable and testy Admiral Hyman G. Rickover, creator and guardian of America's devastatingly powerful sub-surface nuclear strike capability, and notoriously defiant of control by his nominal superior, Chief of Naval Operations Admiral Elmo R. Zumwalt. The Admiral abruptly dismissed my explanation about the need to satisfy Parliament in our democracy saying that, if we did not want the US Navy to defend Australia that was fine by him and, as a *coup de grace*, after listening to us he saw no reason why they should be shouting us lunch. As between umbrage and laughter, I thought the second was the better.

But Schlesinger was more diplomatic than his blunt sailor. Barnard was able to reach useful understandings on other subjects as well. They included clarification of the agreement on the Naval Communications Station.

Barnard had further exploratory talks about the acquisition of the American patrol frigates—the first launching of which was late in 1979.

Barnard made two other journeys overseas. With a need in prospect to order a replacement for our front-line fighter, Barnard decided to examine Sweden's *Viggen*. It was not high in the Air Force's preference. Perhaps sympathy with the country's Social Democrat Government may have been an influence, just as the Labor Government felt some affinity with West Germany's Social Democrats. While in Sweden I was offered a flight to neighbouring Denmark to visit my distant relatives but put the temptation behind me. Barnard visited some other defence plants in Britain.

He took on this long flight a BAC-111 aircraft from the VIP flight. Given its seating capacity he was able to include wives of officials and his own family. Despite our exclusive occupancy, it was not a restful flight. The machine was restricted to about four hours in the air and it landed us in odd places at odd hours for refuelling. By a similar flight, accompanied by his officials and their wives, Barnard visited Indonesia to deliver a patrol boat and later visited the Air Force units at Butterworth and other places in Indonesia as we returned to Australia. Barnard treated his senior officials and uniformed officers like family.

Other decisions for Barnard

Following Barnard's return from the United States, the formalities of a revised North West Cape agreement with the Americans were concluded. He announced several decisions: the intended location near Duntroon of a Tri-Service Academy originally endorsed by Fraser as Minister but put aside by the Gorton Government; the revised threat assessment that I described earlier; and the intention to adopt my recommended reorganisation after preparation of draft directives, arrangement with the Public Service Board and preparation and eventual passage of the necessary legislation.

Labor's new settings for its defence policy were now in place and were, in my view, a formidable achievement after 18 months in office.

There were other decisions reflecting Labor's social philosophy. The civil defence organisation was converted into the Natural Disasters Organisation for relief work in the community as required. Army support for school cadets was terminated (readily accepted by us, as this charge on the Defence vote showed no evidence of later delivering recruits).

He was keen to revitalise the volunteer Citizen Military Force. He established a Defence Force Ombudsman and pushed for better housing for the rank and file.

New problems for the Defence Department under Labor

Some unpredicted decisions by the Whitlam Government had created practical problems in organisation—particularly the sudden abolition by Whitlam of the Service Departments which had been headed by Barnard as a temporary measure. The action had the consequence, presumably unforeseen by Whitlam, of removing the Secretaries from the Service Boards, leaving direction of each of the Services solely in the hands of uniformed officers. In due course the Secretaries were relocated outside Defence, save for Sam Landau. I commented in Chapter 1 on the inadequacy of reporting to Canberra on defence policy debates in Congress and elsewhere. Indeed I had felt in earlier External Affairs days that the Americans served their Australian ally well enough with their views and their information about third countries, wanting no doubt to win our support where it mattered. But we were not doing enough independent studies on the Americans themselves. I never seemed to have enough embassy staff to remedy that deficiency. A similar situation existed in Defence in the 1970s. We needed to read the potentialities for change in American strategic policy and posture. Pentagon sources, cooperative in other areas, were unlikely to offer speculative opinion or forecasts of changes of this kind. In addition, we needed more contact with divergent views in Congress and in the think-tanks that are influential in the United States. Few Service officers were equipped for this kind of enquiry and judgement. More often than not they seemed to approach the Pentagon as a place for sharing operational and professional interests, and for keeping alive past associations in combat.

This attitude seemed to be reciprocated by the Pentagon because, when I nominated Landau to be Defence Attaché, there was an indignant protest and a threat not to cooperate with a civilian. I insisted on keeping Landau in the post. But his wings were clipped. Fortunately, Defence needs were met to some extent by some Foreign Affairs officers with particular aptitude in this field who happened to be in the Embassy.

Reforms of varying merit were being applied throughout the Public Service. We had to fight off some that showed ignorance of Defence requirements. One was the planned creation of a centralised government purchasing agency for the purpose of exploiting the Government's muscle against suppliers—a project with an ideological flavour, pitting the Government against the private sector. A report by a business adviser commissioned by the Government confused procurement by identifying it with the act of purchasing. Doing so (in the case of Defence) failed to accommodate the various elements that entered the procurement process and selections, preceding the purchase contract with a supplier. Big ticket items such as aircraft, ships, sensors, and fire control systems are not bought ready made like motor vehicles on a display lot. Procurement involved an iterative process between an officially approved Defence requirement and the equipment suppliers who showed themselves to be technically capable of producing in a required time scale, with an assurance of maintenance feasibility and much else, in a process involving hundreds of defence experts. Some worked almost as part of the production process in the United States or Britain or France, particularly on the modifications that the Australian buyer required because of the unique atmospheric or geographic features of the continent. There was no such capability elsewhere in the Public Service; and the concept of an adversarial relationship between supplier and purchaser confined to price is inappropriate.

But several years later in 1978 the then Minister, James Killen, announced the scrapping of the system and the restoration of Defence control of procurement processes. His explanation (in succinct terms not always employed by Killen) was as follows: 'Presumably my colleagues opposite reasoned that a civilian Minister, having nothing to do with the defence portfolio, would accept responsibility to the nation for whatever results in war, this socialist apparatus would impose on the Services.'

We had difficulty with the Commonwealth Auditor-General's failure to recognise that some procurement of high technology still in development required management of the inherent risks, which he should judge on that basis rather than simply calling into question the costs implicit in delivery delays as a result of unforeseeable problems in the development process. That said, prudent supervision by the Department of Defence required it to judge when a Service's ambition to acquire the highest technology used by major allies (rather than, as they would say, 'buying obsolescence') involved unacceptable cost risks. Debate on this issue in the Department's policy committees was frequently heated, and was a major contributor to the recurring complaint by the Service users of interference by the civilians. To deplore such Service-civilian tensions as avoidable missed the point. The issues required that there be tension, provided it was constructive in purpose. What was needed in those early days of invigorated Defence Department authority was respect for the different criteria brought to the discussion, and tolerance of people doing their duty. Unfortunately, these emollients were often absent in the debates during my time as Secretary. There were personality faults on both sides.

While we were engaged and stretched to the limit in managing the ongoing programme, and while I was personally tied up in devising Defence Force control for the Minister for Defence, a major investigation of programmes and priorities in the civil Departments was underway. The individual who had much to do with recommending and planning for Whitlam was H.C. 'Nugget' Coombs. This remarkable man served Prime Ministers on both sides of politics and was, in my estimation, the greatest of all those who served the national interest in several capacities, all of them outside of politics. This admiration had been first forged when I had earlier been his subordinate in various international endeavours.

Those investigating the Departments called me up for an investigation. Coombs was not one of them. They were mainly members of the new breed of Ministerial advisers/promoters. Typical of the culture of the times, several were consuming beer while asking their questions (and in one case wounding my vanity by declaring that my opinion would not satisfy an economist). I explained our in-house process of reviewing against policy criteria, the Service and defence factory programme. There is a suggestion in Coombs' autobiography that he was not satisfied by whatever he learned from his advisers in this process (and I was not invited to meet him directly).[8] His memoir reflects his chagrin at not being able to examine whether Defence priorities were adjusting to the new strategic outlook (which of course was precisely what we were doing for Barnard). Coombs had John Stone, one of Treasurer's most competent investigators, as his axeman, but lamented that, like other Treasury officials, Stone was reluctant to target Defence's programmes. My own reflection, on reading this in later years, was that Stone understood that there was no quick fix in Defence, comparable with cutting fertiliser subsidies or business tax concessions—much simpler than making judgements about the relevance to policy of Service activity. Moreover, Treasury had long been a member of the Defence Committee. We were spared educating the Task Force on these matters, while I was myself at the time absorbed in pulling together the ramshackle system of financially managing Defence activity. Labor's Defence budget in 1974–75 made the first step to conform to the new strategic review that had preceded it. In my career I have had few such reasons to be grateful to Treasury.

Reshaping the force structure under Barnard

The new doctrine of the timing of threats, and Labor's emphasis on the defence of the Continent, started a process of change in the structure of the Defence Force. But it was slow and hardly radical. There was resistance at different levels. Politicians in office are reluctant to mothball low priority equipment when the Opposition and media will protest about loss of jobs. When they had been a long time in office, as the Coalition had, they might be admitting past procurement mistakes of their own.

The Services, for their part, continued to table requests to replace whatever equipment they possessed with technologically advanced equipment being developed by the Americans and Western Europe to match the Soviet Union. The beguilingly innocent expression 'up-date' was part of the Service jargon. There being no incentive for a Service to drop out of competition with the other two for a place in the programme, only effectively disciplined priorities in a programme endorsed by the Minister could, if wisdom and foresight prevailed, mould the components into a force called for by the endorsed strategic outlook.

Along with his second budget in July 1974, Barnard presented Labor's first five-year Defence Programme for the years 1975–79. He endorsed the methodology of the system initiated by his Coalition predecessors. There remained the passage of the reorganisation legislation still in the hands of the draftsmen. Even without it, the authority belonging to the Minister for Defence was now beyond question; but the interpretation of the processes for deciding the priorities, along with subjects such as continuity in management of each of the major weapons procurement projects, remained to be dealt with.

As to the content of the budget, and of the new programme beyond it, the share of the Defence Vote going to manpower continued to rise under Labor's expansionary decisions on pay and to conditions of service, and the increase in the regular Army, which had consequences for other elements of the programme. Capital expenditure—the foundation for the future—remained low in the budget. It was possible to move a greater share into Defence facilities around the country. As an example it was necessary, because of the paucity of effective port facilities along our vast coast, to give the Navy adequate facilities for berthing and provisioning for its short-range vessels patrolling the north and northwest. I had myself observed, during a visit to Cairns, the inadequacy of the berths adjacent to a mangrove swamp and of the on-shore facilities placed in a Chinese laundry.

While preparing for the 1974 budget and in later months, contacts with colleagues in other Departments made me aware of the disputes and constitutional crises developing elsewhere. They included the so-called 'loans affair' and the disquiet over the fiscal profligacy of the Treasurer, Dr Cairns, as inflation grew, while he remained determined to finance all of Labor's social objectives. In contrast, Defence, while subject to the various experiments imposed on us that I have described, was sheltered from the acrimony developing elsewhere, particularly as the assault from the Labor Left abated. Our discussions were internal to the portfolio and involved few Ministers other than our own to bring them under control. Whitlam's support of Barnard was an advantage for what we hoped to achieve.

As for myself, I did not try to ingratiate myself with Labor Ministers and had not done so when they were in Opposition. Some Public Service colleagues were more ready than I to try to demonstrate their political sympathy. Unlike others, I declined to attend Labor Party conferences. I had acted similarly when the Coalition Ministers were in Government. I believed that talking to unofficial groups of private Members of Parliament to satisfy the dissatisfactions of Caucus with their leaders was not a requirement of a public servant. I recognise that being so stiff-necked added to a reputation for aloofness and denied me the opportunity to dispel false ideas about my being wedded to the policies of the previous Government.

Barnard's budget statement described equipment decisions that reflected his view of where our strategic interests lay. He told Parliament that we needed to pay primary attention to 'the surveillance and patrol of surrounding maritime areas' along with concepts and doctrines and the build up of forces with 'a better capability for independent actions in our own neighbourhood'. The Navy was to get more patrol boats, and the Air Force acquisitions relevant to the objective. Under this programme, the Navy's prospect of acquiring a blue-water modern aircraft carrier disappeared over the horizon on a reckoning of absence of strategic need. (Its champions nonetheless were to be rewarded a decade or so later.)

The July 1974 defence debate was notable in two ways. One was the participation of the Leader of the Opposition, Fraser, to criticise the withdrawal of concerns for events in distant places. His shadow Defence Minister, Killen, provided more entertainment than content on the Opposition's policy intentions, save for a warning that the new defence organisation would have to be scrapped in war. There remained the differing emphases—on the one hand on capabilities needed for the ultimate defence of the continent; and, on the other, those needed for deployment in support of the Association of Southeast Asian Nations area and other places where security was deteriorating. With hindsight, it can be said that Fraser's insistence on the need to deal with distant threats (consistent with his views in 1970) was a forewarning of what to expect if he became Prime Minister. But I cannot claim to have given Opposition views much attention when immersed in steering Labor's programme, with no expectation of them losing office in the short run.

It was satisfying to me that the Coalition no longer based the case on the need to attract the support of the Americans under ANZUS. The idea of a more self-reliant attitude, and the expectation of acting alone if necessary, seemed to be taking hold. For example, Bill Morrison (shortly to become Minister) drew on the 1972 Defence Review issued in Fairbairn's time to urge acceptance of the responsibility for defending the continent as the priority.

The Darwin cyclone

Labor's Natural Disasters Organisation was tested by the devastation of Darwin by Cyclone *Tracy* in December 1974. In support of the organisation, the Navy mobilised and transported supplies for reconstruction of the city and relief of its stricken and homeless citizens. The head of the Natural Disasters Organisation (Major General Alan Stretton) flew north and took control during the serious disruption that followed the violent winds and new flooding. Defence doctrine had assured us that the country was immune from unforeseen military attacks by an enemy. But Nature was not so predictable. Ministerial support and directions were made difficult by the dispersal of Ministers around Australia for the Christmas break and the absence of the Prime Minister abroad. Senior administrators (Service and civilian) were absent from Canberra. I myself was recalled from my mountain retreat by a message shouted across the river by a neighbour who had been telephoned. Legal authority for orders that had to be made affecting people and property in Darwin was obscure, but Stretton overcame this problem by force of personality.

Vice Admiral Synnot and I concerted in Canberra in conveying to Stretton whatever advice or instructions were called for. Among other things, we sensed that Stretton's success in restoring reasonable order and confidence among the shattered population had imposed a stress on him. We made a point of being present at the airport when his flight south eventually bought him home (after a decision to stay overnight with the acting Prime Minister, Cairns). He later made his record of events, writing a book and by deciding to publish it while still in service.[9]

A retrospect on Barnard

It was one of Barnard's achievements to carry through radical changes in the control of the Services with so little resistance or evidence of animosity. (Where such animosity existed, it had been directed to a different target.) His success can, on my estimation, be attributed to the response by his subordinates, particularly the Services, to attractive elements in his personality. He was not forceful in stating his views, indeed sometimes rather inarticulate. But the former Tasmanian schoolteacher showed evidence of a strong moral code and respect for propriety (which contrasted with the antics of some of his Cabinet colleagues). He relied on his advisers. He showed courtesy and respect to senior Service officers that perhaps attracted a loyalty to him beyond the requirements of duty. He recognised his limitations. He came into office volunteering candidly to me his own and his Party's lack of administrative experience. This shortcoming did unfortunately reveal itself in his strangely inept management of his two private office assistants and his unawareness of what they were doing. He was vacillating in those early days.

In Parliament he was not a striking speaker, somewhat handicapped by a hearing disability from his days as a gunner in the Second World War. He needed, and received, the support of Whitlam in resisting the campaign from the Left against them over the American connection—in the media, in Labor's policy forums, in Parliament and, as he told me, sometimes in the Cabinet.

Reliance on public servants by Ministers is sometimes misrepresented to their detriment. Barnard brought to his portfolio a range of ideas for change. I should note for example that before receiving my advice that I have been describing, he had earlier published proposals for integrating the Service Departments and giving the Services better direction. On the strategic front he had argued for a withdrawal of forces from Asia and for the contention that 'Australia's strategic frontiers are the natural boundaries' (contained in a Victorian Fabian Society pamphlet in January 1969). Whatever research assistance he might have had, he himself clearly articulated orally these thoughts to me several years later when giving me my riding instructions to come up with concrete proposals and objectives.

It is noteworthy that so much of the Barnard/Labor reforms were kept intact during the eight years of Coalition Government that followed Labor's loss of office in 1975.

Barnard chose to leave for his diplomatic appointment as Ambassador to Sweden after he lost the deputy leadership and before the 1975 crisis which overcame the Government. His successor, Morrison, was not so fortunate.

Some of the early confusions of the Whitlam reign, over objectives and sometimes facts, from which Barnard was not immune, stemmed from the new Government's impetuosity and passionate zeal for reform (some would call it a lack of understanding of what governing the country requires of Ministers beyond conforming to the letter of the Party's platform). A more relaxed timetable (requiring confidence in winning a second term of office) would have avoided some of the tensions and disputes. With more time the reorganisation in Defence could have been more comprehensive, using additional investigators, and could have left fewer problems for the future, whether in the military organisation of the Services, or elsewhere in the defence production and procurement areas that were shut out by the timetable given to me and which had to be left unattended while Barnard and his adviser concentrated on what was achievable.

Whitlam's Royal Commission: Enquiry into Intelligence Services

In 1974 Whitlam had decided to appoint a Supreme Court Judge (Mr Justice Hope), with the powers of a Royal Commissioner, to examine the country's Intelligence Services. It was no surprise to have the Australian Security Intelligence Organisation investigated in view of prevalent doubts, not confined to the Labor Movement, about whether its procedures and judgements on individuals had always been consonant in the past with respect for the rights of the individual. I had had doubts and inadequate responses from the Australian Security Intelligence Organisation 20 years earlier, when I was Secretary of External Affairs.

I thought it a perplexing judgement on Whitlam's part to authorise a person eminently equipped for a judicial finding on matters touching the rights of individual Australians, to investigate and make recommendations on the gathering and evaluation of intelligence about other countries where the individual rights of foreigners were not an Australian responsibility. Problems of organisation and control did exist, and there was a case for examining whether there was efficiency in responding to the actual needs of Ministers, officials, and the Services. These were questions of public administration and not judicial findings, save for the question of conformity to law (and the Crown had its own legal advisers to call on). But this confusion did not deter the Prime Minister, and I heard no evidence that he sought from experienced senior officials advice on the terms for a government-organised enquiry. Politicians find solace in Royal Commissions whose findings are unlikely to do them harm politically, and their appointment silences the critics. When the Hope Report was issued, Whitlam was out of office. I would hazard a guess that some of its findings (to which I return later) would have been uncomfortable for some members of his Party had he been in office and required to accept or reject them.

From my earliest time as Secretary in External Affairs I was carried by my then Minister, Casey, into contact with allied Intelligence Services, meeting their Chiefs in London and Washington, and listening to Casey's enthusiasm for the value of such Services. 'War winners' was his opinion, perhaps reflecting his own recent wartime position in the Middle East. But, nearer to home, I was asked to advise him (and the Prime Minister) on suitable arrangements for supervision of a fledgling external Service that had been set up, whose energetic activities and discussions in Washington and London were causing disquiet among senior Ministers. I had no conviction that it would successfully add to the mountains of information coming to us from overt sources. I was apprehensive that, at a time when we were setting out to break down reservations in Asia about our immigration and other policies, any blunders by intelligence gatherers could be serious.

Greatly strained as we were, coping with recurring international military and other crises in the mid-1950s, I tried to avoid being lumbered with any role for me in this. I was also distrustful of the swashbuckling individuals, relishing some high-level contacts they had made in Washington, who were heading the venture. They appeared to bring about their own demise when Ministers decided to abandon the project. But, after the individuals were disposed of, the project was revived and I was told to create some kind of supervisory role for the External Affairs Department, without being involved in knowledge of any clandestine project. This was squaring circles, and the Charter I drafted was later criticised by Justice Hope. Yet it preserved the constitutional validity of Ministerial authority through a conventional Departmental Secretary, while enabling the Minister to disavow, for diplomatic reasons, knowledge of any cause of complaint by a foreign government. The Charter was applied during the remainder of my service in Canberra—one of my least rewarding duties. Later when I had moved to Defence, I tried to get inter-departmental agreement to have the unit confined to a training role, until it developed adequate expertise in intelligence gathering without risks to good defence relations abroad.

By the time Justice Hope started his enquiry I had several years experience with both the product and (somewhat loose) supervision of the Defence Signals Division, which was concerned (as was later publicly declared) with intelligence from foreign communications and with protection of the security of our own. Use of the assessments of the Joint Intelligence Organisation under its National Intelligence Committee was vital to some Defence decisions, including major weapons acquisitions, whether as to timing or content. The system served very well the requirements of the Defence apparatus and its Minister.

We took it as a duty to answer the Judge's questions. I took control of the Department's responses on policy and opinions about how things worked in practice, although he had in addition direct access to the various agencies. When his Report was supplied several years later to the Fraser Government, I was to learn how little influence my views had made. Various changes that he recommended, in areas where I had administrative responsibility, were not discussed with me.

He had no administrative experience. In Chapter 3 I question the validity of some of his assumptions about how Ministers in Canberra would concern themselves with studying intelligence assessments; I also note the superficiality of his treatment of the extent to which the Services and the Defence Department rely on the credibility of the intelligence assessment process in making decisions on weapons selection and otherwise.

Reflections looking back: Whitlam and the Central Intelligence Agency

In the later months of 1975 another phase of anti-American fervour erupted. This led to a renewal of American concerns about the security from public disclosure of those defence activities known to the Minister and the Department but not made public.

Whitlam it seemed had a deep antipathy to the Central Intelligence Agency's involvement in destabilising left-wing governments. The toppling of the elected (Salvador) Allende Government, and its replacement by the repressive (Augusto) Pinochet military government, in Chile was such a case. The Prime Minister ordered that the names of all Central Intelligence Agency personnel in Australia be supplied to him. No doubt scenting political advantage, he publicly declared the tenant of Doug Anthony's house in Canberra to be a retired Agency employee, and former Director of the Joint Defence Space Research Facility at Pine Gap. As I said earlier, it was not until the 1980s that it was revealed by the then Labor Government that the so-called space research activities at Pine Gap employed intelligence officers; and as explained earlier, I considered it important in Australia's interests, for several reasons, that the Soviet Union should not be informed in this way of the information-gathering functions of this highly classified and valuable facility.

The Prime Minister was about to make a public address in Melbourne and I tried to contact him to warn him about the security implications of his campaign to embarrass Anthony by declaring the former senior American at Pine Gap to be a member of the American intelligence organisation. But I met again the obstacle of my attempt to make contact being filtered by his personal staff. In this case, my attempt was treated with derision and a leakage to the press.

To make matters worse, a ham-fisted American intelligence official, Ted Shackley, in Washington fired off a telex to his contact in our Australian Security Intelligence Organisation, extravagantly predicting serious consequences for Australia's relations which could follow the Prime Minister's disclosures. When I saw a copy I decided that this man's threats were not a matter for concern and that higher level policy people in Washington could be relied upon to hose him down. But I did not count upon the mischief of some person publishing the message, perhaps deliberately using the Australian media to regenerate hostility to the Government's defence ties with the Americans. A few copies were distributed within the Department (and possibly Foreign Affairs) and at the political level. I reported to my Minister by having a copy sent to Morrison's electoral office in Sydney where he and some of his personal staff were located. The Australian Security Intelligence Organisation took the message to Whitlam.

Knowing Whitlam as I did, I did not share American concern, and certainly not their excited reaction, except in respect of one aspect of our intelligence sharing arrangement with the Central Intelligence Agency. The problem grew, unwittingly, out of the Prime Minister's distrust of the Agency, which was widely shared in the Labor Movement. I was not in a position to know whether there was any basis for suspecting domestic interference in Australia by the Agency, this being the responsibility of the Australian Security Intelligence Organisation. But I was completely aware of a fully disclosed Agency activity of benefit to Australia. It was one that would be held to be so by members of government of any political persuasion who were made privy to its nature and purpose.

Our principal Defence Department intelligence liaison was with the parts of the American systems which provided us with intelligence, on a reciprocal basis where that capability existed. The liaison gave us intelligence gathered by technology that we did not possess. Some informed us of the state of the nuclear balance between the superpowers on which stable peace depended.

The Defence Department did not have, or need, liaison with any Central Intelligence Agency operations by individuals working under cover in other countries—the most notorious and, to some, objectionable activity of the Central Intelligence Agency. One of the valuable elements in the Hope Report was certification of the value to Australia of 'close intelligence links with some of the major intelligence agencies in the Western world'. During one of my meetings with the Director of the Central Intelligence Agency, I told him of the burden of popular obloquy that partners had to carry, because of the lack of public awareness of the Agency's work in independent analysis of situations in addition to its covert illegal activities on the ground by its agents which attracted criticism and notoriety. I suggested that he could do more to publicise the difference in the multifaceted activities of his organisation. I have no reason to believe that my suggestion had any practical effect.

The 1975 changes: A new Minister, Chiefs of Staff and 'the Dismissal'

Barnard resigned from Parliament in June 1975 and was appointed Ambassador in Sweden. His place in Cabinet was taken by Bill Morrison who had been Barnard's Minister Assisting (and earlier, Minister for Science). Morrison therefore needed little briefing about the full range of portfolio interests.

My own relationship with him was not new, but subject to a complete reversal of status. Morrison had been an officer in External Affairs subject to my authority. He had taken a specialised course in Slavonic studies in London. I had posted him to Moscow as First Secretary and Chargé (his second posting there). In that post he had attracted the attention of the Soviet system and, following our expulsion of a Soviet First Secretary from their Embassy in Canberra for espionage, the Soviet Union retaliated and declared Morrison *persona non grata* on a spurious charge of breaching diplomatic decorum. Barwick as Minister robustly defended Morrison's reputation and rejected the Soviet claim. But the expulsion of Morrison proceeded.

What followed led me to issue a sharp instruction to Morrison. In the media excitement in Australia over the expulsion, Morrison was met by the media at all staging points of his exit. He so clearly enjoyed talking to the media and the light of publicity cast on him that I told him while *en route* to Australia to cool it or, more precisely, to shut up. While the Minister was dealing with Parliament, and I with the Russians and the media, with the truth of the matter as best we could ascertain it, it was necessary to avoid inadvertent conflict with what was being uttered by a distant voice off-stage. What I failed to detect was a budding politician enjoying being a public figure. He left the Department in 1969 after successfully contesting a Sydney seat for the Labor Party. He had had a remarkably rapid rise to the Ministry in the Whitlam Government, holding several portfolios.

As a subordinate of Morrison the Minister, what I had said to him in 1963 did not appear to have affected our official relations. Unlike most of his predecessors, he was well informed on international security and defence issues. He took me and others on the customary call on the Pentagon and other American officials. He investigated the US Coast Guard Service, prompted by the current strain on our naval patrol boat capabilities caused by the flow of 'boat people' into Australian waters. He also examined progress by the Americans with the light frigate programme.

Back at home, the Defence Reorganisation Bill was debated in the Senate in August and on 28 October the Governor-General approved the Act and directed that it be proclaimed and enter into force on 9 February 1976. But before then events were moving into a crisis for the Government.

Morrison's 1975–76 budget sought an estimated 2.8 per cent of the Gross Domestic Product. It reflected the increased cost of Barnard's earlier decisions on manpower and conditions of service, as well as the price inflation which Labor's fiscal policies had generated throughout the economy. Nevertheless, an increase in capital equipment's share was achieved.

But in late 1975 the Government was forced into finding ways of paying for government services as supply dried up under the Senate blockade. Treasury initiated a plan for paying members of the Services with vouchers, redeemable at banks. It was unworkable. An example of this was the situation in which wives and dependents of the Navy's other rank seamen, away at sea, found themselves—unfamiliar with banking and fearful of what might happen next.

Before this bizarre, but constitutionally significant, situation developed further, 11 November arrived. I had no knowledge of the Prime Minister's intentions or, indeed, of any of the political manoeuvres leading to that day. I attended the Remembrance Day service at the Australian War Memorial, returned to my desk briefly, and went to lunch, returning to my office before 2.00 pm. I remained in complete ignorance of what was going on at Yarralumla, and have since relied, years later, on the details provided by Paul Kelly in his book.[10] While I was sitting at my desk catching up with accumulated papers, my secretary burst into the room to say that the Prime Minister had been dismissed and replaced by Malcolm Fraser. This seemed so improbable that I asked where she had received the information. 'From my mum, listening to the radio,' she said. I told her, no doubt with some acerbity, not to interrupt me in future with tales from her mother. Nonetheless, I switched on the radio. I heard Malcolm Fraser speaking from the Government benches. I do not recall whether I gave my secretary the apology for my disbelief that she undoubtedly deserved.

ENDNOTES

[1] Tange's draft at this point stated 'Three installations …', but there is no other indication that he intended to refer to another facility, such as the Naval Communications Station at North West Cape in Western Australia.

[2] Tange's draft at this point referred to 'our Northern region'.

[3] Barnard's Ministerial statement on 'United States Defence Installations in Australia' is at *Commonwealth Parliamentary Debates*, vol. H of R 82, 28 February 1973, pp. 67–70.

[4] This quotation comes from a speech by Kim Beazley, Minister for Defence, entitled 'Checking the Arms Race: Australia's role in international verification' on 13 May 1988.

[5] Alan Reid, 'ALP left looks for scapegoat', *Bulletin*, 3 March 1973, pp. 17–18.

[6] Lloyd became the founding professor of the journalism school at the University of Wollongong. His books included *The Last Shilling* (a history of repatriation, with J. Rees), *Parliament and the Press* (a history of the parliamentary press gallery), and *Profession: Journalist* (a history of the Australian Journalists' Association). He died on 31 December 2001.

[7] Bill Morrison succeeded Barnard as Minister for Defence in June 1975, and was in turn succeeded by James (later Sir James) Killen in December 1975.

[8] H.C. Coombs, *Trial Balance*, Macmillan, South Melbourne, 1981, p. 304.

[9] Alan Stretton, *Soldier in a Storm: an autobiography*, Collins, Sydney, 1978. Tange tried unsuccessfully to prevent Stretton from publishing this book while still in government service.

[10] Paul Kelly, *November 1975: the inside story of Australia's greatest political crisis*, Allen & Unwin, St Leonards, NSW, 1995.

Chapter 3

The Early Fraser Ministry

James Killen, Minister for Defence

Before retirement in 1979 I served my remaining four years in government service under James Killen as Minister and Malcolm Fraser as Prime Minister. At the end there was a well-intentioned, but publicly controversial and financially impractical, proposal from Ministers that I accept an extension beyond the compulsory retiring age of 65, which I declined. On retirement, I was able to turn to neglected family affairs, some writing and occasional involvement in seminars, and to take a short-term appointment nominated by the Prime Minister to review the Public Service in Fiji for that Government.

Killen had held the Navy portfolio (now defunct) in the McMahon Ministry. After the now familiar formalities of inducting a new Minister into some classified areas which were subject to limited access, my first interest was to ascertain whether the reorganised system, and the policies put in place by his Labor predecessor, would be confirmed or wound back. Several matters hung in the air. Although amendments to the *Defence Act* had been proclaimed, they were not to come into effect until February 1976. The content of the Five Year programme would need to be reviewed by the Government, along with its underlying strategic assumptions. We could expect a call for a comprehensive review of those assumptions. Recommendations expected from the Hope Royal Commission affecting Defence would require decision. There was the Defence Force Academy project, several times deferred. There were inefficiencies, such as the low productivity of the civilian workforce in the Williamstown Dockyard managed by the Navy, which needed fixing. The Department had the problem of the over-manned technical and support staff which had been dedicated to the long defunct rocket programme at Woomera. I needed also to learn from the new Minister how he would respond to the unabated sniping from his backbench over the role of civilians in the Department.

Killen confirmed that the Coalition would not try to unwind the system embodied in the legislation. But he wished to place above it a Defence Council chaired by the Minister. I had the documentation prepared. My own attitude was that it was not really necessary to have a Council for him to call in the Secretary and the Chiefs to report collectively to him, but there was no harm in it. Unlike the kind of executive Board of Management for which some Chiefs had hankered, and with which Killen was familiar in his Navy portfolio, such a Council could not be reconciled with the new legislation establishing new lines of authority downwards from the Minister through the diarchy accountable to him. A new Council could advise the Minister but not make decisions. In the event it met rarely.

Problems to overcome in the new system

The time had come to work out arrangements and procedures between the Secretary and the newly created office of Chief of Defence Force Staff in the exercise of their joint administration of the Defence Force. At the same time each Service Chief, now possessing sole command of his Service, had to be given the financial and other delegations needed for him to exercise this comprehensive responsibility, acting within the policy parameters bid down from the Department.

Within the Department it was necessary to give practical shape to the several 'organisations', described in my Report, in the form of conventional Public Service establishments—in most cases divisions headed by First Assistant Secretaries under a Deputy Secretary. I obtained the concurrence of my Service colleague, General Sir Francis Hassett, with this new structure of functional Divisions overseeing uniform policy application to all three Services. Some were headed by two-star Service officers, some by civilians. For example a new Facilities Division, to which I appointed an officer who had originally been a Defence Scientist, would programme the construction and maintenance of buildings and facilities at Service bases. In this way I intended to bring under supervision specifications which sometimes were the product of ambitiously creative Works Department architects, with no incentive for economy, and base commanders seeking nothing but the best for their headquarters. In contrast, living quarters for soldiers' families in Townsville and elsewhere in the North lacked amenities, as a result of earlier Treasury control requiring the Services to conform to the standards of State housing commissions.

The new situation facilitated the setting up by the Department, without tedious negotiation with independent Services, of project teams to manage the acquisition of capital equipment whose procurement and performance specification had previously been approved elsewhere in the system and endorsed by the Minister. It was not so easy to find qualified Service leaders in this field, and thereafter to prevent the loss of the expertise they acquired as a result of their Service's promotion or posting policies that took them away to other duties. We had other frustrations, working subject to the rigidities of different portfolio authorities outside Defence. While approving contracts with overseas suppliers involving large financial implications (larger than likely to be found in the private sector), and with the need for them to conform, subject to penalties, to strict Service specifications, I was denied having legal advice at one's elbow. The indivisibility of Commonwealth legal opinion required that we take time to inform and consult another Department, and to accept the Attorney-General's

Department's own priorities for use of staff. External consultancies were not easily approved as an alternative.

With the disappearance from each Service of the two-star Board members, each of whom had responsibility for managing the specialised area under his command, new lines of authority from, and accountability to, the Chief of Staff had to be drafted. Some archaisms remained to be eliminated at some stage, such as the Army's persistence with semi-independent regional Commands in state capitals—a hangover from pre-Federation colonial days. The Navy, formerly commanded by its five-member Naval Board, was now to be made unambiguously responsible to the Chief of Staff. I left these matters to the Chief of Defence Force Staff. I later came to recognise that I had made an error of judgement in not scrutinising the systems the Chiefs were setting up, where they involved matters of finance and defence policy and not military command of training and deployment alone.

Various misunderstandings or challenges from the Chiefs had to be cleared up or disposed of. The Chief of Air Staff of the time challenged the concept and practicability of 'two-hatted' arrangements. More importantly, the Chief of Defence Force Staff in 1976 stated his view that, on most matters, senior civilian and Service officers should be responsible to both the Chief of Defence Force Staff and the Secretary. This view was unacceptable because the Government had approved my concept that such civilians would remain responsible to their Public Service head, but 'responsive' to the Chief of Defence Force Staff. Conversely, it had been agreed that Service officers under command would be 'responsive' to the Secretary on matters within his responsibilities. Neither Service command of Public Servants or civilian command of Service officers would apply except by specific assignment, and then would not extend to discipline or conditions of service. With the passage of time, working arrangements between the two joint administrators reduced frictions and worked in the way that I expected and have described in the previous chapter. In order to become aware of causes of dissatisfaction with Public Service attitudes, I arranged to make a call periodically on each Chief for frank discussion of any such problems.

As one Chief of Defence Force Staff succeeded another, I came to believe that there was some reluctance on the part of the occupant of this office to overrule the Chiefs of the two Services to which he did not belong. I can only speculate about the attitude of mind behind this. I do recall that during the high-level committee consultations on the five-year programme involving the Chiefs over which I presided during the 1970s, it was often a senior civilian adviser rather than a Chief of Staff who initiated a critical analysis requiring rejection of another Chief of Staff's proposal. There was one exception—maritime aviation was a subject where such inhibitions vanished, as the historic rivalry between the Air Force and the Navy lit up meetings.

The Chief of Defence Force Staff had a rather small staff, yet there was no obstacle to his appointing more senior people to support the exercise of command over the Services, calling a Service to account to him where justified. In later years, looking on as an observer outside Defence, I have noted the use by Chief of Defence Force Staff (now Chief of the Defence Force) of the power of command to bring about substantial changes in Service Commands. Some of these ideas existed in the 1970s but were not put into practice.

Public perceptions in the politics of Defence

I did not expect that proposals from the Services for weapons better related to Australia's strategic environment, along with the necessary policy decisions, would be achieved quickly. Changes in organisation do not of themselves change policies or underlying attitudes. They are intended to work towards the right policies. But in the public discussion in Parliament, and by the so-called defence correspondents in the media, the purpose of change was largely neglected. Instead, attention was paid to the more emotion-stirring and newsworthy aspects: whether one of the Services was to have a favoured weapons system denied, whether civilians had come out winners in some debate and so forth.

A central requirement remained—to ensure that each Service was preparing for the same wars at the same time and in the same place, as Malcolm Fraser had put it back in 1970. Embedded attitudes, old rivalries and aspirations might take another decade or more to change.

Would the electorate, upon which Ministers depended for survival, also adjust? Unlike most areas of Commonwealth Government activity, defence and foreign policy have a constituency which is founded not so much on material and definable interests as on memories, inherited convictions about friends and likely enemies, along with associated fears and attachments, and some historical myths. Some memories and old faiths lose relevance because of radical change in weapons and surveillance technology; or because Australia's geopolitical environment has changed in directions not shared by the countries who have been our familiar friends and allies. But, on my observation of politics at work, it becomes difficult—particularly on the conservative side of politics—to change defence priorities rooted in the past. Old and respected images, like that of the underpaid self-sacrificing volunteer digger of the First World War, stand in the way of new priorities that make less call today on service to the nation of this kind. But there are public institutions that preserve the past in order to honour it. The leadership of the Services themselves, with proud memories of battle achievements, sometimes find lessons in them which have dubious application to contemporary threats that governments would be likely to accept as justifying a military response. Our Services excel in their mastery of ever-advancing technologies. It will always be more difficult to ensure their relevance to credible threat contingencies. That involves judgement about the unprovable, and the assembly of intellectual resources going outside the Services for verdicts that are well informed and objective—and not always popular.

Differing views on our strategic interests

A principal interest for me was whether the Coalition intended to resurrect 'forward defence' as the strategic basis for developing changes in the force structure and, if so, in what direction we would be expected to look for future potential deployments.

I had chanced my arm in an address to a Summer School at my old University of Western Australia in January 1976. I had then argued that we should distinguish between outbreaks of violence abroad that could not be called a 'threat' (that activating word) to the physical security of Australia, and any events that did; and, as to the latter, countries with the maritime capability to attack Australia were very few, and that we would have adequate warning time.

Ideas similar to this were included in a White Paper which we drafted, with Pritchett making a major contribution, and which Killen issued in his first year in November 1976. Killen recognised publicly that Britain would no longer count as a military power East of Suez, while at the same time paying a tribute to the protection which historically Britain had offered Australia.

The Paper pointed to our limited ability to operate in distant places, and to the requirement for successful defence in areas closer to home. For this we needed a force capable of expansion, with a substantial capability of operating independently of allies. I believed we were making progress in two respects: realism about the limits of our capabilities, and abandonment of the earlier public position that a policy of greater self-reliance would throw in doubt the faith, necessary to preserve publicly in the conservative view, that the Americans would bring combat support under ANZUS if Australia needed it.

At much the same time, both the Prime Minister and Foreign Minister Andrew Peacock were speaking of the dangers in the Indian Ocean from the developing Soviet presence and the disappearance of the old power balance. Peacock also pointed to the Soviet Union's achievement of nuclear parity with the United States. When the Prime Minister began publicly defining the threats against which Australia should prepare, I doubt that he was much influenced by the Defence Department's focus on where we believed our essential interests lay (along with its realistic view of our capability of serving them). I did not know whether Fraser consulted Killen, but the content of Fraser's statements confirmed that the Prime Minister was little influenced by the argument in the White Paper that Australia's concern should be restricted to any threats developing in Australia's geographic neighbourhood.

In 1976 Fraser made a number of visits overseas, presumably wanting to convey a policy outlook different from that of his much travelled predecessor. In July he visited Japan and China. His report spoke optimistically of the prospect of a better understanding with China, while expressing apprehension about the build-up of Soviet military strength. He declared it was a concern of Australia that no power would dominate either the Indian Ocean or Southeast Asia.

This focus was different from the Defence Department's concern with our immediate archipelagic North and with the constraints on our capability to deploy beyond our shores. Our difficulty in supporting physically our modest deployment in Vietnam made the point. Stores and maintenance facilities were concentrated in the South of the continent. Means of transport were limited. The constraint was also political: electoral resistance to providing manpower by conscription until a crisis situation was recognised, by which time adequate training might not be feasible.

Yet, in the face of these predictable handicaps, our political leaders have sometimes had a yearning to create an Australia somewhat larger than life and to make political commitments that would be difficult to live up to militarily—whether in Commonwealth Heads of Government meetings or in communiqués with leaders of countries visited. Political and moral exhortation is one thing; being prepared to take military action is quite another. There was a welcome note of self-reliance in Fraser's omission of ritualistic statements of our dependency on the content of the ANZUS Treaty. But he was consistent in his convictions about Australian activism. When Defence Minister six years earlier, in the first declaration of his outlook towards Southeast Asia and the surrounding Pacific and Indian Oceans, he had said: 'If that environment is going to change we want to be able to play a meaningful part in the change.'

In 1976 and 1977 he was reiterating a long-held distrust of Soviet intentions. When later the Soviet Union invaded Afghanistan and enlarged its Indian Ocean naval presence, his reaction was to acquire an aircraft carrier with blue-water capabilities, accepting the claim that such vessels make on financial resources for the escort protection they provide.[1]

Offering defence commitments beyond the military capacity to meet them is not new in the world. British diplomacy has long practised it. For Australia a similar diplomacy or yearning for an international role carries the risk of being left exposed, because an imprudent deployment is not easy to reverse without a price. Deployment abroad engenders national pride. But withdrawal, if made necessary in the face of danger because of being left without allied support, would have the opposite effect and becomes difficult for any government.

I had earlier seen a risk of this kind in the continued retention of the Air Force squadrons at Butterworth after the British had withdrawn from the area and our aircraft on the ground were only protected from close-range guerrilla attack by a not yet effective Malayan Army. In 1969 Prime Minister Gorton had said that their retention made it easier to deploy other units if the need arose, which begged the question whether this vulnerable deployment had strategic value for Australia. My view did not prevail. The withdrawal was made years later.

Fraser was using new people to advise him, particularly on the global threats from the Soviets. In respect of the Indian Ocean as a source of threats, statements by Peacock provided perspective, reminding us of the vast oceanic distance separating the Soviet base in Berbera from Western Australia. It seemed to me, however, that Australia had a more credible interest in the choke points in our archipelagic North than in more distant Soviet locations.

President Carter and the Indian Ocean

The Indian Ocean came under discussion in mid-1977 when Malcolm Fraser made his first call on US President Jimmy Carter. By then the Americans had advocated that they and the Soviets accept a limitation on their respective presences in the Indian Ocean, maintaining a balance but at the lowest practicable level. Australia supported the idea. I do not recall whether there was any Soviet response. At the same time, the Soviet Union was waging a diplomatic offensive by developing its SS-20 medium-range missile capability against North Atlantic Treaty Organization positions in Europe, while simultaneously proclaiming the virtues of a détente in East-West relations which was attracting some support in world opinion.

Later during the 1990s high Russian officials of that earlier period admitted to television interviewers that détente had the specific intention of attracting public opinion, particularly in France, away from support for the American deployments in Europe. One official ruefully admitted lack of coordination with this political propaganda, in as much as the military industry sector chose this time to make the threatening deployment of the SS-20.

I thought it one of Carter's woollier foreign policy forays, when he expounded the idea of making the Indian Ocean a demilitarised zone. Hearing him advocate this to Malcolm Fraser as an appeal to world opinion to offset the advantage of the Soviet case for détente, it occurred to me that the President had chosen for the experiment in disarmament the most distant location from his own territory.

In the diplomatic discussions it had been recognised that demilitarisation confined to the Indian Ocean did not address the potential for a build-up of aggressive air capabilities on the littoral to the Ocean. Pentagon officials began to espouse the idea of an agreement to prevent superpower forces from being so deployed. Australia was one of the littoral states potentially affected. I had discussions with the Pentagon (and, as it proved necessary, with our own Foreign Affairs Department), explaining the impracticability of the idea. I sent Pritchett (who was later to succeed me as Secretary) to explain Australian defence interests. In formulating the Department's attitude I pointed out to our Foreign Affairs Department what the domestic political consequences might be if, in a Senate election, the voters of Western Australia were told of an agreement that forbade the Americans deploying, in an emergency, on their exposed coastline while Queenslanders suffered no impediment to the return of the Americans to their State.

Détente continued to gather some support in the foreign offices of the world and among peace-loving people. I cannot claim to have discerned at the time how specifically it was aimed at destabilising support in France for the American presence in Europe. But in discussions in Canberra I did warn against allowing détente to become the kind of defence soporific that the Soviet Union intended it to be.

As is well recognised, Carter imported judgements about morality into his foreign policy. We had a direct experience of his personal devotion to practising his religion: we waived diplomatic immunity to allow his Secret Service access to the Australian Embassy Chancery rooftop to protect him on Sundays while Carter worshipped in the Baptist Church adjoining our building.

Inflation: Its consequences for Defence in the 1970s

Much of the Department's activity under Killen and the new Coalition Government from 1976 onwards was aimed at bringing to fruition the reforms initiated by its predecessor, and fighting for funds predicated in the ongoing Five Year Defence Programme. The programme under Labor had substantially moved towards a greater share for capital equipment and capital works on bases and fixed installations around the continent.

The days of Ministerially directed reforms were behind us. One reform whose origins preceded the Whitlam Government was the programming system now embedded in the management of the Services and of the activities of the Department. But its methods, and the priorities it recommended for Ministerial incorporation in his approved programme, continued to be challenged by Services whose equipment or manpower bids were reduced or denied under the discipline of the system. In addition, new strains were imposed on the system from the fiscal controllers in the Government as it began to address what threatened to become dangerous inflation. The Consumer Price Index, a standard measure of inflation, grew by 9.3 per cent in 1977 and tight fiscal measures still left it at a high growth of 7.8 per cent in 1978. A practical consequence of this, affecting me and others, was to spend very much time in conference with the Chiefs revising, reprogramming and debating where the axe should fall—time which could otherwise have been spent in addressing deficiencies in various parts of the sprawling Defence empire.

Moreover, I would surmise that this frequent recasting of plans, necessitated by the unwillingness of Ministers to provide budget funds at the level previously approved for planning purposes, fed into doubts about the legitimacy of the system. With a receptive audience among those backbenchers with a Service background, scapegoats could be found—particularly the role of civilians in assessing and disputing plans for their part of the total force structure put forward separately by each of the three Services.

Before long we also began to experience the Fraser style of directing the business of government, and the extent to which he subjected his Ministers and their officials to an inquisition as to what they were doing, and as to the validity of the policies they were recommending to Cabinet. In the main, the Defence Department and its Minister got off lightly, apart from cuts in expenditure aggregates, until the 1978–79 budget. I do not recall any Prime Ministerial intervention in the shaping of the force structure (this was, as I understand it, to change later when, after retirement, I was no longer privy to what went on). Fraser was directing his enormous energy, and his demands on others, to reforming the machinery of government and to meeting the economic and social problems of Australia. We nevertheless felt the backwash of his demands for re-examination of advice, and for a response to demands for information under short and sometimes unreasonable timetables. Some Parliamentary Committees noticeably began treating public servants more peremptorily than had been customary. The style was catching.

Towards the end of 1976 I used a session of the Minister's new Defence Council to tell him that unreasonable strains were being imposed on both civilian and Service officers from the expenditure controllers of Cabinet in the campaign against inflation, and to request his intervention. We had particular problems when Cabinet demands began to be directed at designated expenditure activities without an understanding of the consequences. I believed that some had more to do with pandering to popular prejudice than with achieving rational economies. Cuts imposed on travel expenditure were such a case. Rather than preventing suspected high-living in luxury hotels, the cuts impacted more on the ability to send Servicemen to places where they could train with others in suitable formations, or on the ability of auditors to travel to the remote areas where expenditure delegations were exercised and waste might occur. But we had limited success in getting a hearing.

Beyond these irrationalities on particulars, Defence had eventually to accept a reduction of previously approved programmes *in toto*. In explaining to Parliament the 1978–79 Defence appropriation, Killen was obliged to explain that budget stringency had forced the rescheduling or modification of acquisitions planned in the White Paper two years earlier. He was nevertheless able to point to the transition of the Services to the new technologies of missiles and sensors which had particular value for a country where manpower was limited and had vast areas requiring protection. It was particularly satisfying to the Department that he linked the acquisition of some specified equipment to the requirements for operations in Australia's near neighbourhood—the focus we were advocating. He spoke of patrol boats with an improved sea-keeping capacity for deployment off-shore, and of the stipulation that contenders for the major fighter replacement should have an air-to-surface capability against hostile shipping in the approaches to Australia.

In making his March 1979 statement to Parliament, Killen accepted the Department's advice to marry an emphasis on ability to defend ourselves against credible threats to our own soil with, as he put it, 'the practical option of contributing to Pacific defence in accordance with the ANZUS treaty'. As to the first, he said that our allies could be expected to look to Australia 'to be reasonably self-reliant, and to make a maximum effort to look after its own security'. For me this was a satisfying recognition by a Minister of a conservative government of the outlook given shape by the earlier Labor Administration. Since he was at the same time announcing reduced expenditure targets, Killen went to some lengths to explain that few powers possessed the capability of overwhelming our sea and air forces at the end of a long logistic line, and that most of them are friends and allies.[2] Lesser regional powers did not possess the capability to succeed; and, were they to set out to develop it over time, the intention would be blindingly obvious to us.

In later years, under a succeeding Labor Government, this view of ample warning time came to be challenged as being over-sanguine about the strength of potential local threats. But I saw a cause for satisfaction in that, subject to the ebb and flow of simplistic political rhetoric, there emerged at last a consensus that Australia should make defence of its own territory the first duty of a self-respecting nation without looking first to others.

Differences with the Royal Commission on Intelligence

Early in 1977 Mr Justice Hope began to issue his findings and his opinions on organisation. His Second Report made findings on security checking and a security appeals tribunal—matters involving the balance between individual rights and care for national security. As an administrator I welcomed the clear judicial definition of where responsibility lay, a matter which had troubled me in respect of some cases that arose in my dealings from External Affairs with the Australian Security Intelligence Organisation almost 20 years earlier.[3] The Judge's recommendations cleared away a fog of uncertainty on these matters.

His Third Report was of a totally different character, reflecting the mixed bag of subjects given him by the Whitlam Government. It dealt with the machinery for the official control, direction and coordination of Australia's Intelligence Services (all of them concerned with Australia's interests internationally). As one finally responsible for the administration and funding of several of the Services, I was deeply interested in the Judge's opinions.

I saw no reason then, nor do I now, to treat them as judicial findings, based on evidence and the application of the law. The rights of individuals were not involved. Some laws were relevant (such as accurate use of appropriations) but only marginally to what was a complex administrative matter requiring judgement of how Ministers and officials operated, how they used the system, and how, on the basis of reliable administrative experience, they might operate in future. Working habits could in practice be more important than strictures as to how Ministers and officials ought to use intelligence.

I thought some of the Judge's ideas on these aspects to be inept and his proposed structures (with one important exception) misguided and faulty. As to intelligence-gathering from covert sources, I had long held the view that more information was being fed into the system than would be used by a power possessing interests and influence internationally as limited as those of Australia in peacetime. We had inherited from the Second World War a large and generally efficient collection system, working in collaboration with two great powers, equipped to reveal any threat to strategic interests in any part of the world. But in the post-war world, Australia's activities narrowed as we defined for ourselves a regional rather than a global focus. At the same time there remained a need that was intangible, to assist our partners by gathering information that was of use to them by way of reciprocity for what they provided to us. My opinion on putting limits to our efforts had to be qualified by this consideration. Limits could only be a matter of judgement. The Judge did not share my doubts. His reports called for more and not less intelligence-gathering.

What was needed, in my opinion, was an understanding of how Departments and Ministers and Services operated in Canberra in practice, as distinct from theoretical ideas founded in a constitutional view of the role of Ministers. There is an attraction towards creating new administrative machinery to satisfy requirements that owe more to theoretical pre-conceptions than to hard-nosed prediction of actual usage.

As to control of the covert agencies, there had always been the problem of how to arrange a chain of accountability to someone accountable in turn to Parliament. One agency was responsible ultimately to the Department of Defence while the other (with an undeclared source of funds) was under the general policy direction of the Minister for Foreign Affairs.[4]

For the system of interpreting and issuing assessments on the material provided by the gatherers, there was the opposite problem. To which single Minister should they be accountable? The existing organisation was the product of the Fairhall/Bland administration. The Minister for Defence was accountable through his funding of the National Intelligence Committee and its staff, while the Minister for Foreign Affairs could make demands on the body for priority reports through his Department's representation on a supervising National Assessment Committee. The two principal customers thus had their interests satisfied.

This conclusion necessarily had to be reviewed by the Judge when he took the didactic view that other Ministers and Departments ought to make use of intelligence reports on economic and commercial subjects. The system of control would have to accommodate them.

I thought his basic assumption to be wrong, having long observed, and heard, the preference of leaders of the economic Departments to rely on their own overt sources and contacts abroad. As to Ministers, their long periods of absence far from Canberra, their working habits when spending four days in Canberra, and the competing claims on their time made it extremely unlikely that reading intelligence reports would claim their attention except on rare occasions.

The Defence and Foreign Affairs Ministers were different. The existing system satisfied both Departments. It had replaced an earlier ponderous Committee system based on British practice with which I had had difficulties in External Affairs 20 years earlier. It had provided little aid to policy decisions because of an inability to keep time with the need for a prompt response to, sometimes public, international developments. The current Joint Intelligence Organisation/National Intelligence Committee system had the further advantage of having qualified staff with proximity to their policy customers able to task them with explanations of what they were interested in—thus avoiding the ever-present risk of the intelligence community cocooning itself in a world satisfying its own interests.

As I shall suggest, the Judge's alternative system failed some of these tests of suitability as far as the Defence Department was concerned. In one respect his recommended system had the virtue of breaking away from overseas precedents by devising a system to meet Australian needs. But I believe there was probably a lack of understanding of the differences in the focus of assessments needed in the conduct of foreign affairs and those needed for decisions in the Defence system. Foreign Ministers and Departments are expected to respond promptly (and not lag behind the media) to new events and situations abroad. When there is no crisis of a security kind directly affecting Australia, the Defence system is more likely to need assessments looking to the longer-term future. The process does not demand a Ministerial response. He needs to know that the subject is being worked on for incorporation in later decisions. Emphasis on the longer range derives from the criteria for weapons procurement and training in their use. All require best estimates, at decision time, of the nature of military threat and of the most effective response 10 or even 20 years hence—such is the lead-time, and the time in service, of what is procured or trained for.

The Defence system therefore must have confidence that those making the assessments which will underlie decisions on force structure bring to bear expert knowledge, a reputation for balanced judgement, and an understanding of what studies will be relevant to shaping the force structure. In making his recommendation that 'the greater part of the Joint Intelligence Organisation be transferred to the administration of the Department of Prime Minister and Cabinet', the Judge failed to acknowledge these requirements. His suggestion that an officer of one of the Services be seconded to the new organisation indicated his lack of understanding of the need of the Services to be associated in the way I have indicated. A single Service officer divorced (physically and organisationally) from the Defence system would be a piece of ineffective tokenism.

In December 1976, Killen criticised in Cabinet the proposed demolition of the Joint Intelligence Organisation. Cabinet charged a Committee of senior executives with recommending a way of effecting sensibly the broad purpose of a central assessing and evaluation body responsible to the Prime Minister, without endorsing specifically any part of the Hope Report. I made my objections and criticisms known and this prompted the Prime Minister early in the 1977 New Year to telephone me from Nareen.[5] He directed that we meet shortly to discuss our differences on how to reform the assessing organisation, saying he was not wedded to any particular solution.

Nevertheless, as Cabinet had already decided to create new machinery, in the several meetings that I had with Fraser I could only argue the case for retention of an effective Joint Intelligence Organisation and suggest the restraints needed on this new creation. We met on one occasion for two hours. As to the first, I explained the futility of the idea of satisfying the military and defence requirements of a broad spectrum of intelligence for weapons procurement, as well as military operations, by seconding a single Service officer to this new body. I said that if that body was to enter these fields, the Prime Minister might have to explain publicly why the Chiefs and their supporting Department should rely on the priority given them, and the judgements made by people they had no part in appointing, had probably never heard of, and who were accountable to a different Minister. I also said that my earlier experience made me sceptical of the Judge's expectation of useful commercial information from clandestine sources.

I said there would be a danger of empire-building unless a ceiling was put on staffing, and the numbers of quality people available were few. I suggested 50 or 60 would be adequate. A Joint Intelligence Organisation with functions reduced, but recognised as serving diverse Defence needs, would cooperate with the new body that he wanted.

In what followed these views appear to have prevailed. The Office of National Assessments was kept to the functions and staffing limits that I advocated. During my remaining years at Defence, the two organisations developed cooperative relations including sharing of secure premises. In later years I heard suggestions that the Office of National Assessments was occupied more with distributing assessments of current events affecting Australia, as against the longer-range view of potentialities needed by Defence. This I believe to be more demanding on the quality of assessors because it depends on sound judgement as much as reliable information.

Experiences serving Malcolm Fraser

There were various occasions abroad, not all concerned with Defence policy, when the Prime Minister required me to accompany him. His activities abroad went beyond matters of strategy and the increasing military build-up by the Russians. His Government took the view that Australia's resources of uranium, at a time of growing dependence on electricity generation from nuclear plants, gave us a bargaining counter. Thus armed, Malcolm Fraser decided to tackle the European Economic Commission over its restrictions and subsidies that were hurting Australia. He first visited governments in France and Germany. Although defence matters were not on the agenda, save for a call on the Supreme Allied Commander Europe (General Alexander Haig—later US Secretary of State), I was included in a party of officials, headed by Fraser's 'can-do' Departmental Secretary (Alan Carmody, a former trade official). In an atmosphere of frantic activity, serving the Prime Minister's demands for up-to-date briefings, this was a visit to Europe like no other. In each capital we saw little beyond the walls of hotel rooms where the team wrote papers at night, not on the country outside but on the one about to be visited next morning. In Brussels I was given a seat at the table of a European Economic Commission meeting headed by the President (Britain's Roy Jenkins) and listened to our Prime Minister wade into the Commission (on subjects for which I had no current responsibility). There was much agitation on the part of several Commissioners. It was not my function to ascertain when back in Australia what results ensued. I came away with the distinct impression that Fraser's brusque diplomatic methods in a formal European environment might have been more likely to shock than to persuade.

Back in Canberra, there was not much reason for the Defence Secretary to see the Prime Minister direct. We had had that close association in 1971 and 1972, at a time when he had few confidants and when he needed to talk while he was weighing up whether his dissatisfaction with Gorton should cause him to resign. I have reason to believe that he then trusted me, and some public references to me in later years bear that out. But I did not seek to take advantage by asking to see him when he was Prime Minister. One Minister urged me, as a person he believed the Prime Minister would listen to, to tell him of the discontent among Ministers with the demands he was making on them by taking so much business into Cabinet for them to be grilled in lengthy meetings.[6] Since the way the Prime Minister managed his Cabinet was none of my business, I took no action on the matter.

In 1976 Fraser called me in to express concern about what he thought to be a loss of respect in the Public Service for political impartiality. There were leakages to the Opposition and media of classified documents. This was a time when he was demanding high standards of propriety among his Ministers (and some lost office for various reasons). Over lunch for the two of us in the Cabinet ante-room, he asked me to accept appointment as Chairman of the Public Service Board on the retirement of the incumbent Sir Alan Cooley, apparently believing I could guide the Service back to its traditional standards. In a second meeting I asked him not to pursue the idea. I said I doubted whether I had the necessary good temper for negotiating with the unions over the pay demands then in process (he seemed amused and unimpressed by this). But, more important, I wanted after some years of strain to keep open the option of early retirement, which was an option I would have to forgo in order to do justice to such an appointment. He was understanding. I expressed support for the appointment of Sir Keith Shann, one of our most able Foreign Affairs officers, when his name came under consideration.

Fraser confirmed his confidence in me in various ways despite our infrequent official contact. He had come out in support of me in November 1976 when I was made the target of a smearing claim in the *Bulletin* that the Prime Minister was concerned by the alleged passage of a classified document from Defence to the Russians. The leaked document was one that had in fact been submitted to the previous Government. Fraser testified in the House of Representatives that I had served the Labor Government with, as he put it, 'complete and absolute loyalty', while describing my competence in generous terms—a statement with which Gough Whitlam expressed agreement from the Opposition front bench.[7] I did not look for compliments about my competence, but I was always sensitive to any suggestion of lack of integrity. That attitude was to express itself later when there started a long-running campaign, false and defamatory, suggesting that I had acted, under American persuasion, to warn the Governor-General of the lack of attention to security by his Labor Prime Minister—a subject to which I later return.

There were times during these years when I looked for some relief from the strains of my job. I had never been a good air traveller and suffered from tensions and lack of sleep during so much official travel. I took opportunities for recuperation. On a visit to England I was able to escape from London for a long weekend to stay at the headquarters of a famous trout fishing club (the Houghton) on the River Test. It was too good to be true: mown verges on the stream, no ti-tree to foul the backcast, the river manager to point out which of the abundant trout was worth a cast and which were only two or three pounds and unworthy of the effort. One companion turned out to be a former Secretary of State for the Colonies under an earlier government (a member of the Lords, whose name I do not recall). We talked about some of the African colonies, which he had seen through to independence, and my own experiences in New York when British policy was under attack.

In 1976, early in his term of office, Fraser made the customary call on the US President in Washington (at this time President Gerald Ford, following Richard Nixon's political demise). Fraser and his small party were made guests at Blair House, notable for its comfort and the elegance of its period American furnishings. I was made a guest at an elaborate White House banquet in Fraser's honour attended by a mixed list from officialdom, the stage, and Hollywood. I found myself talking to Gregory Peck about Australia and about the actress Ava Gardner's memorable comment, when making a film of Nevil Shute's *On the Beach*, that the city of Melbourne was a suitable location for a film about the end of the world. Peck said she was very contrite about that, but I authorised him to tell her that, as a Sydney-sider, I entirely agreed.

Having dealt with some intelligence and other defence matters, Fraser set out to discharge an earlier promise by Gough Whitlam to present a cheque for the establishment of a Chair of Australian Studies at Harvard University. Although I had nothing to do with the project, Fraser took me along. After leaving the Carlyle Hotel in New York, where we overnighted, we became aware of a wild storm along the East Coast, which was disrupting planes and generally creating havoc with transport. A notably impatient man, Fraser was not pleased by delays and uncertainties of this kind. We eventually arrived in Boston late after a turbulent flight, and Fraser joined his hosts in a modified programme of which I was not part. Indeed the principal task I was given was to avoid getting separated from the party that would later have to move swiftly for the take-off of Fraser's plane bearing him to Canada. I lunched and had useful conversations with some Harvard academics. I was left with the impression that Harvard did not really need our money, and that a less affluent Ivy League University might have been a better choice. Afterwards I fell asleep in the charming guest-house which had been put at my disposal. Awakened by domestic staff, I was told that the Australian party had long gone on their way to the airport, along with my means of transport. With some help from a student taxi-driver, I made it and caught up with the Australian party, now stranded and unable to leave while the storm continued.

Drama continued at the otherwise deserted airport. Fraser boarded his aircraft, which then taxied to the centre of the airfield and sat immobilised hoping for clearance. Meanwhile the Australian Ambassador in Washington (Nicholas Parkinson) and I had been given unrestricted use of the Delta Air Lines lounge, bereft of staff or passengers, but agreeably provided with self-serve refreshments which we were urged to accept. One solitary stranded passenger eventually appeared—an inebriated man yearning to return to his wife in Florida whom, as he told us many times, he loved very much. Into this touching scene came an airport official conveying a message from the aircraft captain that our incarcerated Prime Minister was now demanding to be let out, and that he now intended to fly back to Washington. There was dismay in his Ambassador's face. But after further time elapsed Fraser did take off for Canada. Now relieved from further duty, Parkinson and I resumed our enjoyment of the available hospitality. A considerable time later a rescheduled flight was given a clearance and Parkinson and I were able to return to more sobering official talks in Washington.

A refuge in the mountains

Early in the 1970s I acquired a property among the mountains in the Yaouk Valley. It was to give me a river, which was its western boundary, for trout fishing, a longstanding passion. It was also to provide an escape at weekends from the demands of someone who has figured in this narrative (and remains a friend to the present day)—the then Defence Minister, Malcolm Fraser. Progressing from primitive camping expeditions, using hazardous tracks in bad mountain weather, we erected a durable log cabin with facilities. It was delivered to the site in a 'knocked-down' condition, despite numerous obstacles, by an intrepid local carrier. Thereafter its erection was undertaken by family, friends and a remarkable local, German-born carpenter. We laid the concrete base on a hurried weekend visit from Russell. My daughter carted gravel, others tended a diesel-driven concrete mixer, my wife shared the smoothing and finishing of the concrete, while I carted water. My carpenter later completed the roofing and the interior, assisted by more weekend visits by me. When working alone, he reached the site by crossing the river in an old vehicle that I left permanently parked by the river for his use. When the river was impassable for a vehicle, he removed his boots, forded the river and made his way on foot. I raised a large granite fireplace and chimney to provide a sole source of heating. Various civilised amenities were later added.

Relevant to this story of my Defence associations, I was now able to invite overseas visitors, such as New Zealand's military Chiefs and Britain's Permanent Under-Secretary of the Ministry of Defence, Sir 'Ned' Dunnett, for fishing excursions. Likewise my Chiefs of Staff colleagues came from Canberra on day visits, and when General Sir Francis Hassett had a minor breakdown in health I cared for him there over several days of a holiday period.

Once beyond the ranges separating the Australian Capital Territory and the Yaouk Valley, rank and orders of precedence dissolve. Personalities with rank, when encountered by the locals, are judged on local terms. I saw this lesson learned by the then Chief of Naval Staff, Vice Admiral Sir David Stevenson, who was berated by a fierce woman on horseback for closing a gate through which she was mustering cattle on their way to her property adjoining mine. On another occasion it was appropriate in local terms that I remained seated in my vehicle while my passenger, General Sir Arthur MacDonald, dealt with gates and waded waist-deep in a swollen rivulet, replacing sleepers in a washed-out culvert, when he came to spend a day in the country. My genial road makers, who often came with their bulldozers, liked to address their city-bound employer and his wife as 'young Arthur and young Mrs Arthur'.

Later in the 1970s, when the incumbent Governor-General—first Sir Paul Hasluck and later Sir Ninian Stephen—came to escape the formalities of Yarralumla, I telephoned neighbours to ask that these dignitaries not be obstructed in any way *en route* through their properties. None objected and I sensed that they did not see the point of the request. There was a potentially more serious obstacle when Malcolm Fraser with his security guard came to visit to fish in the late 1970s. I rang around similarly. I informed a down-stream neighbour that I intended to put the Prime Minister on the river on the property between us, the owner of which I knew was away but who was sure to approve. But the neighbour I consulted was on guard, having promised to eject intruding fishermen. He was unmoved by my protest that the Prime Minister of the nation was entitled to some deference. More out of consideration of me as a neighbour than of the visitor, he proposed a somewhat Irish solution: 'All right! Just tell him to keep his head down so I can't see him near my place'. Given Fraser's great height this was a bizarre request that I thought it best not to pass on to him.

The ability to escape to 'Koonaroo' was not irrelevant to my being willing to carry on at Russell. Persistent resistance to reforms and sniping from Coalition backbenchers against civilians in the Defence Department caused me bouts of nervous tension from which I needed relief.

Despite the absence of a telephone, I could always be reached with some ingenuity. As recorded earlier, when Cyclone *Tracy* struck Darwin in 1974 a neighbour was roused by telephone and shouted across the river over the noise of the rapids that I was to interrupt my holiday and return to Canberra.

Years later, when Chinese forces crossed the border into Vietnam, Fraser demanded my presence at a meeting to be held in the Cabinet room on a Sunday to assess the situation. While my wife and I were clearing obstacles along a track through the mountain at the back of Koonaroo, we were startled by the sudden appearance of a police car. Fraser, never to be denied, had ordered that the Cooma police be sent out to bring me in. After a circuitous consultation by the Constable's two-way radio via Cooma as to how long it would take me to drive back to Canberra, compared with the despatch of an Air Force helicopter to try to find my property, return by air was decided on. My wife was left to make her way to Canberra by 4WD while I answered the Prime Minister's call and attended the Parliament House meeting. It was an occasion when some hosing down proved desirable. I was able to support our Joint Intelligence Organisation analyst (Brigadier John Baker, in later years to become a much respected Chief of the Defence Force)[8] in arguing that a full-scale invasion was unlikely and that the Chinese move should be treated as a blunt warning to the Vietnamese. Subsequent events supported this judgement.

I turn now to some selected areas of reform that were different from questions of strategy and the administration of the three Services. They were the application of science and of advanced education, each in its own way vital aids to a modern fighting force.

The Defence Science Laboratories: Management

Although the defence science laboratories had been brought into the Department, in the 1974 reorganisation neither their status nor control had been satisfactorily dealt with.

There were inherent problems, some arising from geographic dispersion and others from confusion as to whom they were serving. Moreover, the interests of the scientists themselves had to be considered. There was a feeling among some that they failed to receive the acknowledgement from the rest of the scientific community that their achievements deserved because, unlike others, they did not publish papers open to appraisal. Defence security precluded publication of work they were doing on electronics and its application to offensive and defensive weapons, sensors, methods of surveillance and much else. Moreover, their interaction with American and British work in the defence field required strict precautions against unauthorised disclosures. Sympathetic leadership was needed, not merely discipline over their use of defence resources. An objective basis on which to determine what research should be expanded, and what curtailed or terminated, was often hard to find and open to argument. There was the familiar contest between pure research and the application of science to definable outcomes serving defence.

In respect of staff originally deployed at Woomera and in Salisbury to support the British ballistic missile programme, now abandoned, we worked out a programme of retrenchment and transfers only to be frustrated by some timidity at the political level. It was further experience of the curbs that existed in those days on the managerial freedom of a departmental Secretary—lacking power to recruit or retrench or promote or transfer without the concurrence of some external authority.

Farrands brought life and energy into the office of Chief Defence Scientist. He contributed to policy advising in Canberra and I believe he enjoyed respect in the laboratories around Australia for his leadership.

In 1977 I took a closer look at the system. This coincided with Farrands' appointment to head the Department of Science and my appointment of a replacement. He was Professor Tom Fink, Dean of the Engineering Faculty of the University of New South Wales. Fink had a proven record in the application of engineering to the solution of marine propulsion and other areas. I took advice and preferred him over a scientist chosen from the laboratories, while believing that there were some younger men who would be eligible in time (as later proved to be the case).

During visits to some of the laboratories I detected a preference, apart from that for the pure research conducted in some, for serving requests from the Services for aid in problem-solving such as curing defects, or extending the life of equipment. But the Department itself needed advice of a different kind, such as on current acquisition projects, and was not sufficiently in control of priorities in the laboratories. This was a hangover from their former attachment to the Supply Department, with its attitude of independence from the Department of Defence. The urge for independence surfaced in the hopes of some scientists to become part of a statutory body, presumably to decide its own priorities. But to be separated from the users of scientific advice would be a rejection of their *raison d'être* and fatal. It had no support from me.

Management called for judgement on other aspects. There was the familiar tension between claims for pure research and the application of proven knowledge to practical use, in which the former was at risk of losing out in the competition for staff and funding.

In 1979, when the Government decided that all government science should be reviewed, two Defence inquiries were initiated into activities in science and technology. One was an externally directed study to establish the level of scientific quality of this Defence activity; the other was a review by the Department of the utility to it of the resources being devoted to this area. Following these reviews, the entire staff was embraced into the Defence Science and Technology Organisation, within the Department but with its own sense of corporate cohesion.

Members of this Organisation contributed, in ways of which the public could not be aware, to the possession by the Defence Force of equipment tailored to the distances, air and sea temperatures and other physical features, many of them unique, of the continent and its surrounding oceans and air space.

Planning the Defence Force Academy: Obstacles

I earlier described the origins of the concept of a single tertiary-level institution for educating selected cadets from all three Services. For a decade I pursued the objective with determination because of a strong conviction of the need that I have described earlier for more tertiary-educated officers. On more than one occasion when addressing assembled officers, I said that civilians like me were needed for our experience in government policy matters, but that the way was open for us to be displaced by uniformed officers as and when they satisfied Ministers that they had an adequate understanding of the theory and principle of democratic government administration over and above the professional skills of their Service.

I also had a belief that joint operations between Service personnel in combat would be helped by recall of camaraderie and joint endeavours of officers during cadet years. I was influenced in this belief by discussions in New Delhi with Indian officers engaged in the 1965 war with Pakistan, who told of the ease of informal communication during the crisis between those of different uniforms who had lived and studied together.

Existing educational standards among officers nominated for policy positions, or for overseas courses of study such as the Imperial Defence College, were, in my opinion, seldom high enough. The deficiency was compounded by Service practices of various kinds. The accolade of being a 'graduate' was conferred too loosely after attendance at a course of seminars without examination. There was a recurring confusion between training and education—between learning how to do things (often technologically complex) and reasoning about objectives and consequences and the fundamentals of society.

Apart from the engineers in the three Services, the number of graduates was low. But to increase the number by requiring attendance at a new single institution met one obstacle after another. Some difficulties described were real; others sprang from scepticism about the advantages of liberal education at a high level, or from an unwillingness to disturb existing arrangements with some Universities in certain disciplines.

In responding to these objections I had to acknowledge the strong and respected tradition of the Army's Duntroon. I did not think it profitable to advocate with the Chiefs the need for a system of dissipating the loyalty of their tribesmen towards them in favour of a sense of belonging to a single Defence Force.

All three Chiefs wanted assurance that their cadets would remain in an environment in which essential disciplines were enforceable as to conduct and decorum and respect for authority, as well as producing the physical training to test adequacy for the rigours of combat.

There was also the practical problem of how best to relate the educational curriculum to concurrent initial Service training appropriate to the aspiring sailor, soldier or airman. For the Air Force, there was the particular problem of when to undertake flying training and how to programme that unique training in with a normal University-level curriculum. Flying training taken only at the beginning of a three- or four-year course was unacceptable because the skill would be lost by the time the cadet graduated.

The Chiefs stressed the all-important requirement of leadership being inculcated. During one session with them they began to question what the curriculum of academic studies would be. We were not presumptuous enough to believe that we, rather than academics, would decide the detail, but I agreed that the question was a valid one, up to a point. When 'man management' was suggested, I said I doubted if this was a tertiary subject and said 'what about philosophy—it gets you asking questions'. The ensuring silence implied that I had made a poor joke. The Air Force wanted primarily engineering and science. I tried to steer them towards making room for their cadets to have their minds open to the humanities.

These questions were matters of policy, in my opinion, and not to be left to the academics' views of their responsibility to this unique cadre of students, however much they might (and did) talk about freedom from interference on academic matters. I was in yet another minefield of professional egos. On a learning visit of my own to the Faculty of Military Studies at Duntroon, I learned from some academics that I belonged to a breed called 'bureaucrats'.

I accepted the Service view that, apart from some unavoidable use on cost grounds of civilian academic courses in some specialisations (such as engineering), joining the campus of one of the major Universities, with the cadets housed in some sort of barracks, would not provide the required disciplined environment. When I suggested that there could be advantages in broadening contact with ideas developing in the civilian world, and other financial advantages, if a quota of civilian students were enrolled in the new institution, one of the Chiefs growled: 'long hair and thongs!' I did not press the point. This was the 1970s, with the libertarian 1960s still fresh in mind. Slowly we found solutions that matched Service needs to an academic environment, and also wore down outright opposition from some quarters.

But then we encountered the resistance from outside. It came from some Universities and some vice-chancellors. When the Fraser Government announced its intention to give the institution the status of a University named after the distinguished Richard Gardiner Casey, the vice-chancellors started to revolt. The Vice-Chancellor of The Australian National University, Professor Anthony

Low, came to see me several times to warn me of the likelihood that his colleagues would be sparing in their cooperation. There were doubts about matters of scholarly independence in a military based institution, and so forth. I entertained the thought that other motives might be at work. Was there room for a new rival in Canberra? Would The Australian National University continue to be denied an engineering faculty while the new institution would have a well-endowed one? While unspoken, these motives might be there. When, in the event, the idea of a separate stand-alone institution was given up, the opposition of the vice-chancellors was largely dispelled.

While Labor was in office, a Defence Force Academy Council was set up under a former Vice-Chancellor of the University of Adelaide, Professor Sir Henry Basten, to plan the institution, using various studies of likely student numbers from each Service and the preferred faculties. Estimates of numbers had to be speculative. Some excessive predictions of numbers with the necessary level of secondary achievement might have been prompted by Service self-esteem.

With Malcolm Fraser now Prime Minister, we had hopes of progress. But it was first going to be necessary to sell the idea to Killen. He in turn would have the obstacle of that group of backbenchers who made common cause with the dogged opponents in the Services to the changes in education and institutions that would be involved.

Nevertheless, we got to the stage of site development, and engaged the National Capital Planning Authority in our projects. I had good support from my colleague and friend, General Sir Arthur MacDonald. I enjoyed his candour about the limitations of civilian advisers. When I suggested on an earlier occasion that some operational activity could be performed at less cost by civilians he had remarked, memorably: 'Two or three civilians can perform a task, but have more than that and you get a rabble.' I was seated beside him at a briefing by a landscape architect who was demonstrating, before a landscape model, the virtues of a siting plan for the proposed academy. The amiable young man elaborated on the care given for the amenities of the cadets by way of shrub-lined paths leading from their quarters down to the lecture halls along which, as he said engagingly, 'they can meander or ride their bicycles'. My neighbour stirred suddenly, then interrupted with the voice of command: 'They will not meander. They will not ride bicycles. They will march!' A clash of cultures, one might say.

The shape of what later became a college of the University of New South Wales owed much to the respect enjoyed by its Vice-Chancellor. Professor Rupert Myers was a scientist, engineer, long-time University administrator, and active in many national cultural activities. He was an excellent bridge between the cultures, and I think he, and I as an administrative reformer, valued each other's cooperation.

Obstruction continued. The Parliamentary Public Works Committee took evidence from some Service officers who were not supporting their Chiefs. After canvassing alternative ways of educating Service cadets, rather than pronouncing on the building project as such, the committee came out against the Australian Defence Force Academy project. The Prime Minister spoke to me, suggesting that they might have gone beyond their charter. I said I entirely agreed and that they ought to stick to discussing bricks and mortar and not education policy. In the event the Government went ahead. A few months after I left the system it announced (in February 1980) that the Academy construction would proceed, and that it would be under the academic supervision of the University of New South Wales. The opportunity to create a University named for Casey, the great Australian who had served at Gallipoli, had had to be forgone.

Australian Defence Force Academy cadets of all three Services have, since the opening, won respect for academic achievements, in some cases of the highest order, while also meeting the exacting standards of military discipline and leadership. It is noteworthy that some of the highest achievers have been female. At the time of recording these recollections I have been informed that Australian Defence Force Academy graduate officers are now occupying responsible policy positions in the Defence Department.

Using soldiers in support of police

In 1978 I received a summons from the Prime Minister to join his advisers at the Commonwealth Heads of Government Meeting at the Hilton Hotel in Sydney. The Prime Minister of India was Morarji Desai, and Fraser was apparently aware that I had got on well with him in New Delhi and could provide a useful contact if needed in Sydney.

I arrived at the hotel to find that a bomb had exploded in the street, killing a worker in the vicinity. The Prime Ministers were due to travel the following day, for the traditional 'retreat', to be held at Bowral. Sir Geoffrey Yeend, the Secretary of the Prime Minister's Department, and the small group of advisers were told by Fraser that he wanted the Army to provide protection along the route, lest the bombing be followed by a terrorist attack on the visitors. He spoke to Neville Wran, the Premier of New South Wales, and it was agreed that the police would not be capable of providing adequate protection against such an event. I was charged with the initial moves to get an Army detachment organised. I recognised that it would be necessary to have legal power vested in the Army detachment to take any necessary steps, such as control of movements of civilians along vulnerable points on the route and the use of military force against any actual threat of violence.

The first was easier to achieve that the second. My colleague back in Canberra, the Chief of Defence Force Staff, General Sir Arthur MacDonald, issued the necessary orders through the Army Chief to the chosen unit at Holsworthy, after establishing what military presence might be needed, the details of timing of movement and so forth. Brigadier John Coates (later a Chief of Staff and scholar)[9] came from Holsworthy to our little office in the hotel to discuss final details of the intended travel, and to indicate the capabilities of his men.

What still remained to be established was their legal power to act against civilians. I was no expert on procedures for authorising military action in support of the civil power (that being the police). Nor, after several telephone calls to the Department and legal advisers, was useful information easy to find. The legal procedures had not been dusted off in several generations. My memory told me they were based on archaic British Army doctrine in British India. The need of legal cover was real. A soldier manhandling a civilian, or in the worst case shooting him without legal cover, could end up in goal. I knew something of the Indian experience where riots from time to time required the Army to be called in to support the police. Indian histories record the notorious case of the wretched Brigadier Dyer, blamed for the massacre of rioters in the Punjab (although most died not from gunshot but by being crushed in a panic).

Instead of squiring Morarji Desai, I was given the problem of providing legal protection for which, together with Yeend, I tried to find answers far into the night. Telephone calls to colleagues in the Attorney-General's Department yielded nothing useful. My memory told me that it had been British practice after a call-out in India to require a magistrate to survey a riotous situation. If the police were unable to cope, he was required so to certify, whereupon warning shots could be followed, if necessary, by open fire upon perceived ringleaders. But, where to find this quasi-judicial process at night in the middle of Sydney? Our small group of officials pondered briefly on the idea of finding a magistrate, possibly in bed or watching television, and presenting him with a bewildering request to authorise a Commonwealth agency to use force if necessary against a resident of his State. The notion collapsed into hilarity while we searched our minds for a more practical solution. One was produced by the Army itself. After formal call-out action in Canberra, Brigadier Coates deployed his detachment along the road to Bowral. For those travelling this route by car rather than choosing to be uplifted by Chinook helicopters, he arranged for police to be available at points where any suspicious action might require a response, the soldiers being a deterrent.

While some citizens of the Southern Highlands might have been alarmed by the appearance in their midst of armoured personnel carriers (needed solely for their communication systems) nothing ever threatened the Prime Ministers, as I was to learn later when back in Canberra.

Thus I returned to Canberra without ever meeting Morarji Desai.

Final months in the Department

James Killen continued as Minister for some years after I retired. During our associations I found him affable and cordial to staff, and courteous to his civilians. One might expect, when visiting his office, to hear about the talents of the racehorse pictured on his wall (just as my first Cabinet Minister 20 years earlier, Casey, liked to talk about the aeroplanes that he flew). Killen took evident pleasure in his association with Service officers whether in his office, on their parade grounds, or in their messes. His strength lay in Parliament where he used his oratorical flourishes and witticisms to change the atmosphere of the House. He showed me personally much consideration. Examples were his insisting that a wall plaque on a new building in Melbourne where he attended the opening should bear my name rather than his; and his generous designation of my wife for the launching of HMAS *Canberra* at the Seattle shipyards.

Killen had his problems with Fraser's style and methods as did other Ministers, one of whom resigned in protest. It was not a case of interference in the Defence Minister's territory but rather locking him up in long Cabinet meetings that denied him the time to spend with his advisers. Whether Fraser was using a commendable process of consultation, as some have suggested, or employing a method of getting his own way by wearing down opposition, is a matter of opinion.[10] My own judgement is that Fraser disliked going out on his own and had to rally supporters. Whether this was the politician or the man I am unable to say.

Some of his Government's decisions were troublesome for defence administration. Although the Government proclaimed a priority for fostering productivity in Australian industry, I encountered long opposition to declaring redundancies in the over-manned facilities remaining at Woomera that I described earlier.

At the same time Fraser supported consistently the reforms in the system with which he had earlier been associated when Minister for Defence, one being getting the Defence Force Academy created.

The gap between the strategic guidance and Defence preparations

When I left the Defence Department there still remained doubt whether the structure of the Defence Force and the deployment locations of its formations were an accurate reading of what the official strategic guidance called for.

I had taken the view that it was for the Services themselves, and not the civilian administrator/adviser, to apply professional judgement to proposing for approval the detailed operational capacities, the particular equipments, the deployment of formations, and the logistics they would use for the kind of combat or deterrence declared to be a credible contingency in the agreed strategic outlook. But the Services, led by the four-star officer in the Department who had command over them, did not fill the void. From time to time they would complain about how the void frustrated them, but it remained.

Nor did Ministers in my time ask questions about the linkage or its absence. I have observed that, long after my retirement, under the direction of a well-qualified Minister (Kim Beazley), the gap was filled by the so-called 'Dibb Report' of 1986. Paul Dibb I know to have been an unusually well-informed officer with experience in strategic assessment. He was aided by a senior Army officer [and two senior-level civilians] and they mustered sufficient military support for the statement of capabilities, and the redeployment of units and assets, that was needed. There was a subsequent redeployment of forces to the North and West, and the mothballing of some equipment.

During his term, Beazley laid down a dictum in terms that civilian advisers had been urging Ministers to impose on the Services during the two previous decades in documents quoted earlier. This was a disciplined relationship between defence preparation and reasoned strategic guidance. In my time we could not be sure that we had unambiguous support where it mattered—the Cabinet Room. It seemed to me as an outside observer of the final years of the Fraser Ministry, at the time of the Afghanistan and Indian Ocean scare, that much of the earlier sober advice not to equip Australia for far-off missions, beyond the likely willingness of the community to support them with manpower and other resources, carried little weight. Perhaps those years illustrate the axiom that it is difficult for governments to change policies because to do so is an inherent admission of past error, to be exploited by the Opposition.

In his Roy Milne Lecture in November 1987, Beazley laid some blame on Defence Department practices for the difficulty:

> Effective defence policy must be grounded in a sophisticated and accurate assessment of our political and military environment but political pressures almost invariably work to favour vague and simplistic fears over careful analysis.

These fears, he went on to remark, prevailed over 'the more highly intellectual presentations that are the usual product from Russell Hill'.[11]

He focused the blame on the closed internal processes of discussion there, while the public debate, with which Ministers were necessarily concerned, proceeded unaffected on its traditional course.

No Minister that I worked for drew attention to the defect in the advisory system. In retrospect I can see that the process, starting with Shedden and followed by his successors Hicks, Bland and Tange (and I would guess those that followed) of deliberating without the presence of Ministers, and thereafter mailing, in effect, the results to them, made an ineffective impact on Cabinet.

Looking back I can recognise other deficiencies in the scope of our inquiries in the 1970s. For example, the process of devising a force structure capable of projecting effective power from Australia, or of using it on our own soil if it came to that, should embrace contingency plans for mobilising the resources (such as transport) belonging to the private sector, and the support of the instrumentalities of government at all levels in the Federation. This for long remained an unexplored field for the Defence Department, perhaps because our history of fighting in the territory of other countries or on the high seas narrowed the vision of what defending our own territory entails in practice.

But I doubt that Beazley (who had a grasp unusual among Ministers that I served) offered a way by which the usual run of Ministers could dislodge popular misconceptions about defence threats. To persuade Ministers to listen to necessarily long presentations by the experts in the field would call for priority over party room, Parliament, constituents, petitioners and many other claimants on a politician's time. Two full-time Ministers are the minimum required, such is the scope of activity for which the Defence portfolio is responsible. And it will be up to the Prime Minister to appoint Ministers not for their ability to beat drums that Servicemen like to hear, but to recognise what the security interest of the country requires. But can they always be produced by the electorate? Putting aside such a counsel of perfection, as history suggests we must, the public will need to support academic and serious media analysts, and to differentiate them from the lobbyists advocating narrow interests, some of whom can be observed in Parliament itself.

Two Ministers will not be on top of all the activities across the country and abroad. As might be expected, I believe Ministers will need a Public Service that is not afraid to supply the memory that few Ministers can have, or to suggest what does and does not serve the national interest, accepting that public servants can be shown to be wrong and may have to be moved if they are persistently wrong or waffle under tension. I also believe that the staff of Ministerial offices, appointed to serve above all the electoral interest of the Minister and the Government (assuming they are always identical) should not, while entitled to be kept informed, condition Public Service advice. Their advice may be parallel, but it should be separate.

Personnel policies and practices in the Services

One reason for the predominance of civilians in the screening of Service bids for expenditure commitments lay, in my opinion, in the failure of the Services to prepare officers for this kind of objective analysis and to retain them in the job with the experience they gained. While in some heated controversies aggrieved Services dubbed civilian investigations to be 'paralysis by analysis', the civilians counter-charged the Services as being too submissive to shiny brochures of the arms manufacturers with their lobbyists in Canberra, and to the attractions of ever-advancing technology with insufficient weight given to cost-benefit. There were doubtless exaggerations on both sides. The civilians strengthened their claim to objectivity by the use of defence scientists, some of whom I transferred into systems analysis. All three Services had specialist engineers to support their bids along with operational experience which, however, did not necessarily equate with analytical ability. Their project officers could not remain long in the job because of the Service practice of job rotation.

To my mind an even more fundamental obstacle to those in uniform becoming perceptive and objective analysts lay in the educational standards accepted by the Services. Their personnel policies (described in Chapter 2) compounded the difficulty. Officers measuring up to the demanding tests of professional knowledge and leadership in the field were expected to become analysts understanding policies in procurement laid down by the Government. I believe that reforms in the educational system for officers have gradually changed this picture. These observations are not hindsight. Frequently, in lectures to senior officers, I personalised the matter by describing the capabilities they needed to acquire if they wanted to reduce the influence of officials like me.

The depth of education (so often confused with Service training) seemed to vary from one Service to another. The Army, perhaps because they were not tied so much as others to managing high technology (in short, modern warships and aeroplanes, and their sensors and weapons systems), seemed to produce officers who had spent more time in forms of a broader education.

These personnel practices in the Services, perhaps particularly how officers were selected for higher rank, deserved more attention from Ministers than they received. When invited after my retirement to address an Australian Defence Force Academy seminar on officer education I said

> Personnel management will be supremely important. When we supplement professional training ... with expensive tertiary education. ... Governments will want to be satisfied with Service management. I have to say that there is no aspect of Service administration so firmly removed from external scrutiny and public discussion. This reclusiveness should be dissipated. I watched with concern the tendency (of one Service) to blow out its brains through age retirement and wonder at the personnel policy that permits this.[12]

Defamatory media fabrications

During the decade following my retirement I was pursued by false and defamatory media accusations about my service in Defence. It was said variously that I had contacted the Governor-General (Sir John Kerr), or required the Chief Defence Scientist (Dr Farrands) to warn the Governor-General that my Prime Minister's actions were imperilling Australia's security relations with the United

States. A more offensive embellishment was to the effect that I had acted at the behest of a foreign intelligence agency, namely the Central Intelligence Agency.

The statements were untrue. At no time did I discuss with Kerr either the actions of the Prime Minister or any aspects of Australia's security relations. The journalist perpetrators were Brian Toohey, William Pinwill and John Pilger.[13]

Toohey and Pinwill had each had privileged access to classified defence information when occupying positions of trust in a Defence Minister's office through which Departmental and Services papers passed on their way to the Minister. Toohey worked in Barnard's office in 1972; Pinwill in the office of Bill Morrison (when Morrison was Minister Assisting from mid-1974 and later Minister for Defence in 1975). He was employed there when the Minister lost office in November 1975 and the Minister's records had to be packed up and disposed of by his staff.

Each of these persons after leaving his Minister's office made a career for himself in journalism writing about defence subjects, including Australia's links with American agencies. Toohey wrote somewhat boastfully in various Fairfax journals about his possession of classified Defence documents from undisclosed sources. By the mid-1980s he had secured the editorship of the Fairfax journal, the *National Times* (later defunct). While less prominent in his journalistic career, Pinwill, as a servant of government, undoubtedly had access to information that he was subsequently able to use in his writing, presumably for remuneration. It is noteworthy that the notorious Shackley telex was sent on my instructions to Morrison's office to keep him promptly informed. That telex from an Australian official in Washington reported a foolish threat from the Americans that Whitlam's actions would imperil continued American intelligence cooperation. The message surfaced in the media and was made the centrepiece of theories by these and other journalists of a conspiracy to influence the Governor-General immediately before he dismissed the Prime Minister.

In 1979 Toohey was pursuing inquiries into links between the Department and Kerr before the November 1975 dismissal. Farrands had had a discussion with Kerr in November that had been arranged pursuant to Kerr's practice, which started (and he had discussed the idea with me and others at a meeting) early after his appointment to Yarralumla, of asking senior public servants to talk to him generally about their work—in this case the kind of work conducted in the Defence science laboratories.

I told Farrands that I did not intend to make any response to Toohey's enquiry about this meeting because I did not trust him to use information without distortion to suit his agenda, and I directed Farrands to do the same. I understand that this ban on Farrands excited Toohey's suspicion.

In early 1982 Toohey began his first attack on my integrity with the statement in the *National Times* that I had arranged for Farrands to brief the Governor-General on the security concerns about Whitlam, and that Farrands had done so. All—Kerr, Tange and Farrands—have denied the truth of what was written. Farrands and I (both then in retirement) independently engaged lawyers to charge the Fairfax press with publishing false and defamatory statements. Both of us said, in effect, that we would not proceed to Court proceedings if we received satisfaction. In my case this was the printing without rebuttal of my letter of denial and payment of my legal costs. My denial was widely published in the more responsible journals. Three years later Toohey sent me a catalogue of questions about contacts between me and American agencies connected with a former Pine Gap Director. I told him to direct his inquiry to the then Minister for Defence, Beazley. A similar request to the head of the Australian Security Intelligence Organisation, Allan Wrigley, received a more acerbic refusal.

In retrospect I recognise that it was an error of judgement to believe that the best way to treat these falsehoods was silence, to allow them to die of inanition, while I got on with a fully occupied departmental life. But this conventional Public Service practice of leaving public discussions to Ministers was not a sufficient protection where one's personal integrity was being challenged. This became clear when the slur sprang to life through the mouth of a television commentator, John Pilger, who is given to finding conspiracies on dubious evidence but often given hospitality by the Australian Broadcasting Corporation and occasionally the Fairfax print media. He was aided by Pinwill acting as consultant. Pinwill wrote at one time a denial of the need for truth in reporting, saying pretentiously: 'Journalism is not a court of law; it is a process of weaving together, often from necessarily anonymous sources, the strands of history.'

Pilger declared a 'senior public servant' to be guilty of denouncing Whitlam's security reliability. Someone in London having used my name publicly, I was asked by the Australian Broadcasting Corporation whether I was the individual. After I warned the ABC to be aware of a possible action for defamation, my name was omitted. I observed, during a later television debate about the ABC's use of Pilger's programmes, that Paul Lyneham of the ABC remarked that 'he had threatened to sue', which is a journalist's way of leaving the derogatory impression that an unpublishable allegation against an individual might still be a valid one. A number of senior journalists wrote pieces accepting my denial.

Post retirement experiences

In the early 1980s Fraser responded to a request from Fiji's Prime Minister, Ratu Sir Kamisese Mara, for an Australian to advise on the operation of his Civil Service Commission. Fraser recommended me for the task. After months of investigation in Fiji my reports, public and private, addressed the lack of method and much elementary incompetence which I found in the way the staff were exercising, or neglecting, their control of departmental establishments and selections for promotion. I saw at first hand the conflict of principle with equity in the opportunities for higher office as between Indians and Fijians, where merit alone would have greatly favoured one race against the other, less educated and agile-minded.

Later the Government gave me the privilege, when an election made it impossible to send a Minister, of representing Australia among the envoys celebrating Fiji's 10th anniversary of its independence. There were appropriately dignified ceremonies to mark the occasion. Britain was represented by Princess Anne, whose conversation revealed a percipient understanding of what was going on in Australian politics. Inescapably, as has been my experience abroad over the years on solemn occasions, there were events that I found less than solemn. The Crown Prince of Tonga, a huge man of seemingly immeasurable weight, was taken on a tour of the University campus. Prudent arrangements had been made for reinforced seats at intervals to enable rest to be taken. Unhappily his guide, becoming distracted, led him off course. Rest was taken but I am told at the expense of much damage to University property as he smashed one conventional chair after another.

Some other hangovers from my Public Service days were less enjoyable. While in Fiji I was pursued by the Privileges Committee of Parliament to appear before them concerning actions, thought to be intimidatory, against an officer who had given evidence critical of the Department and Chiefs of Staff to a Parliamentary Committee. While within public administrative circles I made known my poor opinion of the judgement of this particular whistleblower, I avoided any action that would be contempt of parliamentary privilege. On return to Australia I learned that there had been some heavy-footed and insensitive actions by officers in the Department during my absence. When I did appear before the committee, various propositions were put to me that knowledge of the critical view of the individual by so influential a person as myself had inspired culpable actions against the individual by others in the Department. My recollection is that I displayed due modesty at the implied compliment, but left it to the Committee to find some wrongdoing to pin on me by the indirect route they had chosen. I believe their Report suggests they were not successful.

On serving Ministers

As earlier recorded I had, prior to the 10 years of advising Defence Ministers and implementing their decisions, performed the same duty for several External Affairs Ministers in the course of 20 years beginning in 1943. Allowing also for the Ministers in other portfolios who acted temporarily during the frequent absences of our own Minister, I came to observe at close quarter rather more than 20 of the species.

Each of the External Affairs and Defence portfolios made its own unique demand in respect of policy and the kind of directions needed to be given to subordinates. All were similarly accountable to Parliament for what they did or what was known of what they failed to do.

My own personal experiences with individual Defence Ministers have been narrated in Chapters 1 and 2. In many ways I was fortunate in the relationships that I had earlier in External Affairs. There one had to adapt to differences of personality and style. One or two were most likely to be influenced by forms of approach that I found difficult to adopt. I am not a natural flatterer and this irritated Evatt. Nor did I excel in the kind of acerbic wit, puncturing the arguments of others, that Menzies enjoyed hearing from some of his favourite advisers. My problem was the greater when Menzies uttered excoriating verdicts on some of the anti-colonial and non-aligned leaders of the time. The External Affairs argument for understanding and tolerance of the anti-Western rhetoric of those days rested not on demonstrable facts but on somewhat vaporous arguments about the need to have respect for 'Asian opinions'.

In my first years in External Affairs, Evatt, in his strident and excessive demands on Australia's behalf abroad, made me aware that the family relationship with Britain was no guarantee of respect for Australia's interests. After the 1949 election, direct contact with four significant Ministers in succession (P.C. Spender, R.G. Casey, R.G. Menzies and Garfield Barwick) left a strong imprint on how they expected the Department to respond to international situations and institutions.

Within days of taking over from Evatt, Spender told me of his intention to abandon Evatt's reliance on the United Nations at a time when threatening communist regimes were spreading. Putting limited reliance on Britain, we would turn to the United States for security protection. His stated fears of a resurgence of Japanese militarism seemed unduly pessimistic. We suspected that he was using that argument against joining the soft peace treaty, which John Foster Dulles wanted, to extract a formal commitment from the United States to satisfy our concern for our future security. He achieved what he wanted against the scepticism of his Prime Minister. He had looked to a group of officials (not including me) to marshal the arguments and draft the texts.

Inheriting this achievement, along with the developing hostility of Communist China to a formal conclusion of the Korean War, Casey applied himself to cultivating better relations with the Asian countries emerging from colonial status and declining to be aligned with the Western powers to which Australia was attached. The Department was enthusiastic in supporting him. But he lost out on many occasions in Cabinet, which was clinging to the past and containing some racial prejudices. In the Department we responded to his caring style towards his officers and fully supported his indefatigable activities abroad, but

I doubt that we did enough to persuade him of the need to carry public opinion with him in his endeavours in Asia.

I saw no harm but little prospect of practical outcomes in Casey's well-intentioned advocacy, with his high-level British and American contacts, of a return to the Anglo-American unity that had been crucial in the defeat of Germany. The Department shared his despair at Menzies' support of Eden's disastrous attempt in 1956 to restore British influence in the Middle East after Gamal Abdel Nasser's takeover of control of the management of the Suez Canal.

In contrast with Spender, who allowed no room for officials to share the limelight that was always important to him, Casey made a point of including senior officials in his conversations with world political leaders of the time. I was a frequent beneficiary. His motive was to enhance the status of officers of his Department. He was unlike Spender in another respect. Status, whether social or political, was not something that he had to lay claim to. He had acquired both as a young man. There was no need to give officers notice of his superior status. In the case of one or two who had personal problems he was generous with fatherly advice.

In the mid 1950s, during Casey's frequent absences abroad, the Defence Minister, Sir Philip McBride, acted in his portfolio. Undemanding on policy matters, McBride was another Minister who treated his officials with great courtesy. He was unflappable as well. This I learned when, soon after dawn, I had had to beat on his hotel door to coach him in preparation for an early visit by the Soviet Ambassador bearing an expected protest that we had abducted Mrs Evdokia Petrov on the Darwin airfield earlier in the night. The occasion was her decision to seek asylum from the grip of her Soviet guards on the way to Moscow in order to join her husband who had weeks earlier defected from the Embassy.

With Barwick we had no difficulties in serving his policies, and he had clout in Cabinet. He consulted his Department and enjoyed a debate, usually good-natured. He also enjoyed winning; and more often than not we had a bonus in hearing unsolicited opinions on a surprisingly wide range of subjects other than External Affairs.

Although Menzies was usually avuncular in manner towards his public servants, I was sometimes ill at ease in his presence during my two years with him as Minister. There was seldom any dialogue on matters I brought before him; and when he had approved a Cabinet submission in his name I could not be sure that he would not present it to his colleagues as simply a Departmental view. Perhaps he was already coming to the view, expressed to Barwick a year or two later, that it would be best for me to vacate the Secretary's office.

To influence Hasluck we had the obstacle that, as a former Departmental officer dealing directly with Evatt in Canberra, and having served on the UN Security Council and jousted there with the implacable Andrei Gromyko, he did not believe he needed advice. I believe he had also a desire to rid the Department of any pretensions to act other than under strict instructions, as it had done years before when he saw John Burton acting thus. On one occasion I was sharply told that 'policy is for Ministers'. I did not take kindly to undeserved rebukes of this kind.

Having returned after five years in India to serve under the young Malcolm Fraser in Defence, I admired his energy. Because he tended to jump to unfavourable conclusions without waiting for the evidence, and to be sparing in the advisers he trusted, one could expect arguments with him. In contrast, his successor, David Fairbairn, was passive, stolid and uncritical, taking few initiatives and none to change the ineffectiveness of the weakly controlled Defence system. I have earlier recorded my experience with Gorton and Fairbairn in the twilight of the McMahon Ministry. I had many opportunities to advance my views to the new Labor Ministers when they came into office, although not always in time to try to head off some impetuous intentions of Whitlam in his later months.

Recalling these experiences with Ministers prompts some general observations on the relationship of the Public Service with Ministers in the 1950s, 1960s and 1970s. I discovered that a required art of the official is sometimes to infer policy from a silent or inarticulate Minister—which is not the image cultivated by politicians of a Service whose simple duty is to wait for policy direction and to implement it faithfully. As to those Ministers who welcomed policy advice, some would respond if it were made in conceptual terms. Others preferred the concrete, perhaps because of a canny wariness lest there be unforeseen consequences in generalisation. Perhaps this lay behind John McEwen's opposition, described earlier, to advice from the Defence Committee in 1958 to achieve a greater defence capability of acting without allied assistance. Some intellectually well-equipped Ministers (Evatt, Spender, Menzies) would sometimes formulate policy direction in a dialogue with officials on the principles to be applied. Casey, an engineer by training, preferred less elusive and more concrete propositions and would not have been party to the demand in later years for a more modest policy role for the adviser. He once asked me: 'You show me all the options. But what, for the love of Heaven, do you recommend?' He liked the detail of the Colombo Plan aid in its various forms. As to less tangible matters, the advice to be offered by an official in External Affairs or Defence, for the Government to use in communicating with other governments during the Menzies era, would often have to be derived from the rhetoric of generalisations frequently used by Ministers, like 'support for friends and allies' or 'support for ANZUS'.

In advising Ministers on defence matters, their decisions would need to have regard to public perceptions and not simply material facts (like the state of another country's military capabilities). These drivers would include accumulated popular fears or mistrust of particular countries as well as embedded loyalties to those seen as friends, particularly by Coalition backbenchers who served alongside Britain in the Second World War. The official learned that the driver differed as between the two sides of politics, be it loyalty to the United Nations or loyalty to Britain, or avoiding public disagreement with the United States.

Advising Prime Ministers had a special dimension for obvious reasons. There was no right of approach past one's own Minister (something that Chiefs of Staff had to be brought to accept). Moreover, there was a progressive concentration of power in the office of successive Prime Ministers and its extension into areas belonging to other portfolios. The impact of this on officers of other Departments varied with personalities. There was scope for occasional bullying at one extreme, while at the other Sir John Bunting was invariably considerate in explaining how Menzies would prefer a matter to be handled. Some of his subordinates were not so open about the advice they were privately giving. The view that Casey expressed to me, that Menzies should accept that he use his Ministers as his advisers, had no chance of succeeding.

All the Ministers were scrupulous in not revealing to me any details of Cabinet discussions. When Menzies opposed the more liberal proposals of his External Affairs Minister, Casey would indicate as much to me by well-mannered grimaces at Menzies' name. Barwick, who did better at overcoming Menzies' opposition, would trumpet his successes to me with the joyful cry: 'Thunder on high today!'

The possibilities of advising a Prime Minister while travelling overseas have varied. In those early External Affairs days, with Menzies so unsympathetic to much of the advice we would offer, announcement of an impending Prime Minister's Conference in London, with Menzies on the loose, would be received with some dismay in the Department. Menzies was always considerate towards conventional procedure (while Gorton was not). External Affairs would always be included in his entourage and treated with courtesy. But as to influence on policy in Conference, or in the meetings he had with British leaders, it was negligible. He himself made sure of this. In the Savoy Hotel where we were all quartered in close proximity, Menzies was adept at skipping in and out of his suite without being waylaid by any of the advisers lurking in the corridors hoping to get to him with last minute 'briefings'. He made amends for any injury to *amour propre* by sharing his martinis at cocktail hour, which was not the occasion for badgering him with policy advice.

It comes naturally to a former public servant to argue the virtues of a Public Service that is competent and possesses experience and memory that few Ministers can possess, and the value to Ministers of listening to Public Service advice. Whereas Menzies was confident enough in his Ministry's control of policy to urge his new Ministers to consult and listen to their officials, a later generation became more selective in this practice, apparently believing such dependency was weakness or perhaps open to misunderstanding of the thrust of the Party's policies. As to the intellectual qualification of Ministers, there is little doubt that, as compared with my early days, there has been a marked increase in their academic qualifications (which, however, is no guarantee of better judgement).

In the early 1950s the speed of change in Australia's external environment called for more information and explanation to the public. Unlike later years, the Universities during the years of the Menzies ascendancy of the 1950s contributed little. The practice of Ministerial 'guidance' of the media, with facts and statements of attitudes on external security issues arising from time to time, differed greatly as between Casey and Menzies. Casey bombarded the press with statements that he wrote on matters great and small; Menzies in contrast remained aloof and often scornful of so-called 'scribblers', preferring to make formal statements to Parliament. In like fashion, Hasluck rejected sharply a suggestion of mine that he give daily access to him for guidance by an officer that I had appointed to give non-partisan background information to the media. He professed to be indifferent to what the media chose to say.

After Labor's reorganisation of Defence in 1974, Defence Ministers needed relief from being overloaded, but in a form that preserved central control of policy and consistency in its application in each of the Services. Previously, overload was not the problem. Three Ministers, usually junior from the late 1950s, each supervised (perhaps with differing assiduity) one of the Services; and a Minister of Supply supervised Defence factories, purchasing contracts, Defence science and some international cooperation. The relationship between Public Service and Ministers was significantly affected by Labor's transfer of authority to the Minister for Defence that I have described, along with the widened power of the Secretary.

The problem of overload was exacerbated by the rejection of my advice to place some Supply Department activities elsewhere. The Whitlam Government turned to a device that I had had some part in devising when Menzies had taken the External Affairs portfolio, and had decided to call on another Minister to assist him. He had agreed to establish an exact list of matters upon which the Department would take orders from another Minister (in this case the Minister for the Navy, Senator Gorton). The necessity for this makeshift device lay in Counsel's opinion on the Constitution. This was to the effect that Section 64 did not permit more than one Minister to administer a Department; and that if a member of Parliament were made Assistant Minister, and received emoluments, he would be subject to a severe penalty. In later years the constraint disappeared, after the Hawke Government on different legal advice made dual appointments without challenge.

In the Defence Department in the 1970s, a 'Minister Assisting' had relieved the Minister of some time-consuming matters of procedure and routine in respect of the Services. He was allotted the Service personnel area for policy direction and control. But Ministers Assisting had their public and electoral repute to advance in their own portfolio rather than get involved in controversies elsewhere. The deficiencies in Service promotion policies, described in Chapter 2, and the failure to prepare enough uniformed officers for policy and analytical work, remained. In the absence of Ministerial direction, the practices of the Services carried on as before.

Two conceptions of Ministerial–Public Service relations were held in my time, although put under challenge in my later years and since. One was that the Service would be expected to apply its accumulated experience and its intellectual resources and judgement to discerning where the national interest lay; and to make this the foundation of its advice to Ministers. Along with this went the obligation to implement what the Minister decided, without going public on whether or not the view of officialdom had prevailed. This notion of a closed-circuit relationship later gave way to adoption by Ministers of multiple sources of advice, and to a challenge to the right of the non-elected officials to purport to define where the national interest lay.

A second conception was that assurance of permanency in the career carried an obligation to offer the Minister unpalatable advice where necessary for the public good. Because the Departmental Secretary was appointed by the Government, he could not claim permanency as a legal right, because the Minister must have trust in those who are best placed to know his shortcomings while bound to accept his directions. Silence in public had to prevail, leaving it to the parliamentary process and the media to bring to light half-truths and self-serving evasions. As to that, these methods of scrutiny were not, in my experience, likely to bring to light confusion of mind or indolence or other frailties that afflicted some.

Whether the break-up of the fabric based on these conventions serves the national interest remains to be seen. In matters involved in the defence or diplomatic posture towards rival or potentially hostile powers, which was the area of my own practical experience, I have reason to doubt both the ethics and the prudence of permitting non-public servants who are not bound in a career structure the opportunity to take information gained in the service of governments for use elsewhere serving their own interests.

As for myself, I accepted the obligations that went with having the freedom that prevailed in the early years to advise Ministers in private as one wished. In showing a Minister the respect, in both substance and manner, due to the high elected office that he held, I also expected reciprocity in civility towards me. I had no cause to complain, being too junior, to take offence at Evatt's sometimes bullying manner. A testy encounter in later years with John Gorton (when he was Minister assisting Menzies in the External Affairs portfolio) ended in a draw, which had no lasting effect that I observed in my later relations with him as Prime Minister.

In the matter of relations at the personal level, some of my colleagues seemed to hold the view that too much closeness could threaten the non-partisan standing of the Service. As to this, there was a dilemma when it was a Minister himself who sought a friendly social relationship. While it would be imprudent and perhaps demeaning to court a Minister's friendship to serve a hope of further advancement in the Service, it would be churlish, I believed, to reject a friendly social relationship when offered it. Casey treated his officers as a family (he had been an officer himself), and to some he was appreciative in practical ways of their health or other problems. After his retirement (but only then) he presented several of us with mementos expressing gratitude for our assistance. Maie Casey showed a particular regard for, and was generous to, my daughter.

In the early 1950s Canberra was a dreary place for Ministers far from home. Only a few acquired houses for their family (they included John Gorton, later Malcolm Fraser, and Robert Menzies with the Lodge). Diversions were few, as were friendships in a Cabinet bound together only by the politics and hopes of survival they shared. When Casey, something of an outsider to them, occasionally asked whether my wife would provide him with a grilled chop, we did so knowing how unhappy he was in Canberra. The friendship that existed between us remained long after his retirement.

Some other Ministers may have had a similar relationship with their Departmental Secretary of which I was unaware. In one case of a senior Minister, solace took a different form. He was a hard drinker and gifted raconteur in the evening lounge of the Hotel Canberra, and it was widely believed that the manager of that institution earned his MBE for seeing the Minister into his bed.

I developed lasting friendships with Garfield Barwick and later Malcolm Fraser. I was not inhibited by any sense of departure from party-political neutrality. When Gough Whitlam and Lance Barnard took over, my relations with the Prime Minister were cordial; and likewise with Barnard and his wife, fostered when my wife and I shared convivial times with them after travelling in their aircraft for official discussions in Asia and Europe. This benign attitude to me was not shared by the Victorian Left Wing of the Labor Party, who attacked Barnard for it.

To be a party political eunuch is not everyone's ambition. But in my chosen career it made possible my part in founding, under the Labor Government, a radically changed system of defence decision-making, and afterwards preserving it under a Coalition Government for my successors to build upon in later years.

Reflections on a personal journey

The experience that I brought to Defence, already related, was very different from that of the Service Chiefs with whom I was to work, and whose codes of Service loyalties and responsibilities I had to understand.

As noted earlier, my first international experience was not with matters military but with international plans and organisations in economic, social and, later, political areas. My first encounter with defence and security advice was when North Korea (later joined by China) invaded the South, and the United Nations authorised a military action against the invaders in which Australia joined.

Many people had earlier sharpened my awareness of the interests of Australia in the world requiring to be protected. H.C. Coombs and fellow economists whom I served had campaigned to convince a resistant United States of its obligations to conduct expansive domestic policies upon which the trade opportunities of other countries depended.

Some of my External Affairs experience had limited value in Defence. My financial responsibilities had not been great. My managerial experience had been directed at creating an effective organisation for the Department for the first time; and for assessing the suitability of people for particular responsibilities within it. I had much to learn in Defence (which was not the kind of assessment that came naturally to my predecessor and friend Henry Bland). I had by then formed a view of the Public Service and its disciplined performance that some of my earlier External Affairs subordinates may have found over-demanding. I had a deep conviction that public service was more than a career; that it was a duty to the public.

I recorded in earlier chapters my judgement that the Services were gripped overmuch by the experiences of the past in addressing Australia's present and future. I came to recognise that this was to some extent an understandable product of deep attachments of loyalty and spirit that were fostered by living institutions. In Foreign Affairs it is easier and best to be pragmatic about whether or not to allow traditional friendships to affect policy. Rash misjudgements in the language of diplomacy seldom have long-lasting effects; and time is a healer. But in Defence the lag time in everything is long, and wrong preparations, or nomination of the wrong likely adversary, carry the risk of more lasting damage. Caution about change can be justified.

I had to think again whether the censorious views I had expressed before coming to the Defence Department (noted in Chapter 1) were less applicable to the Chiefs than to the defence organisation, kept in being by successive governments, that preserved rivalries for resources without a disciplined system requiring conformity to government-approved strategic priorities.

The most senior Service officers brought into the Department as Chairman of the Chiefs of Staff Committee or Chief of Defence Force Staff brought an experience very different from that of a chair-bound civilian. My first had British Army experience pre-war and later served in combat with Australians in the Middle East and New Guinea during the Second World War. My second, a naval aviator, had had carriers sunk under him twice. The third had served in combat in the Middle East and later Korea. The fourth had commanded in Vietnam; and the fifth had commanded the Malayan Navy after many sea-going commands. The Service Boards contained officers who had served on the ground or in the air over Europe and North Africa.

As they rose to eminence in the fighting profession, they had one feature in common: with occasional exceptions, they had been commanded by, and been given their strategic instructions by, an ally (Britain or the United States). In 1970, Fraser proclaimed that the Services should prepare their military capabilities from a strategic assessment that was common to all three and accepted by the Government. It was this that subsequently occupied me in getting it articulated and observed in practice. The residual influence of Australia's past associations, going back to earlier Imperial defence, helps explain how much grip the past had on the later response to the contemporary Australian environment. But there was more than that for the civilian administrator to understand. As I see it, the lifeblood of a uniformed Service is loyalty; and when it was directed upward it was directed eventually to Australia's Head of State by three 'Royal' Services. Past campaigns fought under American as well as British strategic direction are honoured; and in addition there are public institutions preserving and honouring past service in these campaigns.

All of this called for respect on my part. But respect could not extend to accepting priority for modernising and replacing equipment and developing capabilities originating in past campaigns against enemies that no longer existed, or which no longer credibly related to this continent's changing geopolitical environment. As I have tried to illustrate in this memoir, my work with the Services was mainly about getting a consensus on what capability was relevant to the future and within the country's realistic willingness to support it; and about persuading Ministers to accept that conclusion. This was unfinished business in my time. And with so many uncertainties always up for judgement and debate, it is likely to remain so.

ENDNOTES

[1] In order to maintain Australia's naval aviation capabilities, the Fraser Government decided to acquire the HMS *Invincible* from the United Kingdom. When the Falklands War broke out in 1992, however, the Fraser Government agreed to permit the UK Government not to conclude the transaction. Alternative options were still being considered within the Australian Government at the time of the 1983 general election. Soon after its election, the Hawke Government decided not to pursue the idea of a new aircraft carrier for the Royal Australian Navy.

[2] Killen's Ministerial statement on Defence on 29 March 1979 is at *Commonwealth Parliamentary Debates*, vol. H of R 113, pp. 1324–34.

[3] This is principally a reference to the case of Ric Throssell. See Ric Throssell, *My Father's Son*, William Heinemann, Richmond, Vic., 1989, and Peter Edwards, *Arthur Tange: Last of the Mandarins*, Allen & Unwin, St Leonards, NSW, 2006, pp. 92–93.

[4] The references here are to the Defence Signals Directorate and the Australian Secret Intelligence Service. The existence and role of these agencies, and the identity of their heads, is now publicly acknowledged, but this was not the case for most of Tange's career.

[5] Fraser's property in the Western District of Victoria.

[6] Tange indicated at another time that this Minister was James Killen.

[7] See *Commonwealth Parliamentary Debates*, vol. H of R 102, 17 November 1976, pp. 2756–57.

[8] Paul Dibb, who also attended the meeting at Parliament House, remembers the Joint Intelligence Organisation analyst (to which Tange refers) as Brigadier J.O. Furner (who later became Director-General of the Australian Secret Intelligence Service) instead of Brigadier John Baker.

[9] John Coates, who was a Colonel rather than a Brigadier at the time of this incident, later became Chief of the General Staff (the position now known as Chief of Army) with the rank of Lieutenant General. After retirement he became a distinguished military historian at the Australian Defence Force Academy.

[10] These questions are discussed at length in Patrick Weller, *Malcolm Fraser PM: a study in prime ministerial power*, Penguin, Ringwood, Vic., 1989.

[11] Kim Beazley, 'Thinking Defence: Key Concepts in Australian Defence Planning', Roy Milne Memorial Lecture, 6 November 1987.

[12] The source of this quotation has not been located. It does not appear in the text of Tange's talk on 'The Education of Officers for Government Administration' to a meeting of the Australian Study Group of Armed Forces and Society in May 1980, as reproduced in *Sir Arthur Tange, Defence Policy Administration and Organisation: Selected Lectures 1971–1986*, a collection of lectures printed in 1992.

[13] These allegations are discussed in the Appendix to Edwards, *Arthur Tange: Last of the Mandarins*.

Bibliography

Ayres, Philip J., *Malcolm Fraser: A biography*, William Heinemann, Richmond, Vic., 1987.

Ball, Desmond and David Horner, *Breaking the Codes: Australia's KGB network 1944-50*, Allen & Unwin, St Leonards, NSW, 1998.

Barnard, Lance, Ministerial statement on 'United States Defence Installations in Australia', *Commonwealth Parliamentary Debates*, vol. H of R 82, 28 February 1973, pp. 67–70.

Beazley, Kim, 'Checking the Arms Race: Australia's role in international verification', 13 May 1988.

———, 'Thinking Defence: Key Concepts in Australian Defence Planning', Roy Milne Memorial Lecture, 6 November 1987.

Bland, Sir Henry, 'Some aspects of defence administration in Australia', Roy Milne Lecture 1970 (published as a pamphlet by the Australian Institute of International Affairs).

Coombs, H.C., *Trial Balance*, Macmillan, South Melbourne, 1981.

Edwards, Peter, *Arthur Tange: Last of the Mandarins*, Allen & Unwin, St Leonards, NSW, 2006.

Edwards, Peter with Gregory Pemberton, *Crises and Commitments: The Strategy and Diplomacy of Australia's Involvement in Southeast Asian Conflicts 1948-65*, Allen & Unwin with the Australian War Memorial, St Leonards, NSW, 1992.

Fraser, Malcolm, Statement at *Commonwealth Parliamentary Debates*, vol. H of R 66, 10 March 1970, pp. 232–47.

Gorton, John, '"Forward defence" or "fortress Australia"?', *Sydney Morning Herald*, 21 June 1971.

Hancock, Ian, *John Gorton: He did it his way*, Hodder Headline, Sydney, 2002.

Holdich, Roger, Vivianne Johnson, Pamela Andre (eds), *The ANZUS Treaty 1951*, Department of Foreign Affairs and Trade, Canberra, 2001.

Horne, Donald, *Into the Open*, HarperCollins, Sydney, 2000.

Horner, David, *Defence Supremo: Sir Frederick Shedden and the making of Australian defence policy*, Allen & Unwin, St Leonards, NSW, 2000.

———, *Strategic Command: General Sir John Wilton and Australia's Asian Wars*, Oxford University Press, South Melbourne, 2005.

Kelly, Paul, *November 1975: The inside story of Australia's greatest political crisis*, Allen & Unwin, St Leonards, NSW, 1995.

Killen, James, Ministerial statement on Defence on 29 March 1979, available at *Commonwealth Parliamentary Debates*, vol. H of R 113, pp. 1324–34.

McNeill, Ian, 'General Sir John Wilton: A Commander for his Time', in David Horner (ed.), *The Commanders: Australian military leadership in the twentieth century*, George Allen & Unwin, Sydney, 1984, pp. 316–34.

Mediansky, Fedor A., 'Defence Reorganisation 1957–75', in William J. Hudson (ed.), *Australia in World Affairs 1971–1975*, George Allen & Unwin, North Sydney, 1980, pp. 37–64.

O'Neill, Robert, *Australia in the Korean War 1950–53, volume 1, Strategy and Diplomacy*, Australian War Memorial and Australian Government Publishing Service, Canberra, 1981.

Reid, Alan, 'ALP left looks for scapegoat', *Bulletin*, 3 March 1973, pp. 17–18.

Stretton, Alan, *Soldier in a Storm: An autobiography*, Collins, Sydney, 1978.

Throssell, Ric, *My Father's Son*, William Heinemann, Richmond, Vic., 1989.

Weller, Patrick, *Malcolm Fraser PM: A study in prime ministerial power*, Penguin, Ringwood, Vic., 1989.

Woodard, Garry, *Asian Alternatives: Australia's Vietnam Decision and Lessons on Going to War*, Melbourne University Press, Carlton, 2004.

Index

Aeronautical Research Laboratories 37
Afghanistan 104, 125
Age (*see under* Media)
Air Force, Australian (*see* Royal Australian Air Force)
Alice Springs (*see* Joint Defence Space Research Facility)
Allende, Salvador 94
America (*see* United States)
ANZUS Treaty (1951) 6, 9–13, 16, 30, 35, 40, 72–73, 90, 103–104, 108, 133
Association of Southeast Asian Nations (ASEAN) 90 (*see also* Southeast Asia)
Attorney-General's Department 100, 123
Audit Act 1901 (*see under* Legislation)
Australian Army 7, 17–18, 21–22, 24–27, 29, 31–33, 35, 38–39, 42, 44, 50, 54, 56, 58–61, 63–64, 70, 78, 80, 82, 85, 89, 101, 122–23, 127
Australian Broadcasting Corporation (ABC) (*see under* Media)
Australian Defence Force Academy (*see under* University of New South Wales)
Australian Labor Party 49, 55, 76, 83, 89
Australian National University, The (ANU) 120–21;
  Strategic and Defence Studies Centre (SDSC) at 39
Australian Security Intelligence Organisation (ASIO) 92, 95, 108, 129

BAC-111 aircraft (*see under* Britain)
Baker, John 117, 140(*n*8)
Barnard, Lance 43, 45–46, 49–53, 57, 62, 68–72, 74–86, 88–89, 91–92, 96–98(*n*7), 128, 137
Barwick, Garfield 11, 13–15, 76, 96, 131–32, 134, 137
Basten, Henry 121
Battle, William C. 30, 47(*n*20), 83
Beazley, Kim 22, 47(*n*15), 52, 71–72, 75–77, 82, 97(*n*4), 125–26, 129, 140(*n*11)
Beijing (*see under* People's Republic of China)
Belgium:
  Brussels 112
Berbera (Somalia) 105
Bhutan, Kingdom of 16
Blakers, Gordon 10, 23, 37, 39–40
Bland, Henry 17–24, 26–28, 31, 33, 37, 110, 125, 138

'blue-water' navy, concept of 21, 39, 41–42, 90, 104
Boeing:
  Boeing *707* aircraft 52;
  Chinook helicopter 123
Booker, Malcolm 11
Border, L.H. 17
Borneo (*see under* Malaysia)
Boston (*see under* United States)
Bretton Woods International Monetary Conference 1
Brezhnev, Leonid 72
Britain 3, 7–8, 47(*n*2), 54, 75, 78, 85, 87, 103, 130–31, 134, 139;
  BAC-111 aircraft 52, 85;
  Centurion tank 81;
  Ditchley seminar 45;
  Imperial Defence College 119;
  London 4, 5, 7, 19, 36, 51, 47(*n*13), 93, 96, 114, 129, 134;
  RMS *Queen Mary* 4;
  Royal College of Defence Studies 45;
  Royal Military Academy Sandhurst 16;
  Savoy Hotel 134
Brogan, Mervyn 61
Brown, Allen 10
Brussels (*see under* Belgium)
Buchan, Alastair 45
Bulletin (*see under* Media)
Bunting, John 46, 52, 134
Burton, John W. 1–3, 133

C-130 *Hercules* (*see under* Lockheed Corporation)
Cabinet of Australia 8–9, 11, 13–14, 19, 25, 27–28, 31, 34, 36, 43, 50, 52, 56, 62, 69, 80, 91, 96, 107, 111, 113, 116, 124–25, 131–32, 134, 137
Cairns, Jim 83, 89, 91
Cairns 89
Cairo (*see under* Egypt)
Canada 114–15
Canberra Times (*see under* Media)
Carlyle Hotel 114
Carmody, Alan 112
Carrington, Peter 13, 77–78
Carter, Jimmy 105–106
Casey, Richard Gardiner 5–6, 8, 11, 21, 66, 93, 120, 122, 124, 131–35, 137
Central Intelligence Agency (CIA) (*see under* United States)
Centurion tank (*see under* Britain)

143

Chairman of the Chiefs of Staff Committee (CCOSC) 26, 32, 35, 39, 52, 57, 64, 66–67, 139
Chief of Air Staff (*see under* Royal Australian Air Force)
Chief of Defence Force (CDF) 58, 102, 117
Chief of Defence Force Staff (CDFS) 58–60, 65, 68, 82, 100–102, 122, 139
Chief of Naval Staff (*see under* Royal Australian Navy)
Chief of the General Staff (CGS) 33, 61–63, 140(*n*9)
Chief Defence Scientist (CDS) 37, 50, 68, 71, 118, 127
Chiefs of Staff 14, 17, 25–26, 56–57, 96, 115, 130, 134;
    Chiefs of Staff Committee 26, 32, 35, 39, 52, 57, 64, 66–67, 139
Chifley, J.B. 1, 50
Chile 94
China (*see* People's Republic of China)
Chinook helicopter (*see under* Boeing)
Citizen Military Force 85
Clark, Alan 55
Coast Guard (*see under* United States)
Coates, John 123, 140(*n*9)
Collins, John 7
Colombo Plan 2–3, 133
Commonwealth Heads of Government (CHOGM) 104, 122
Commonwealth Scientific and Industrial Research Organisation (CSIRO) 37
Constitutionality 3, 25, 53–54, 56, 89, 93, 97, 109;
    Federal Constitution (Australia) 13, 53, 76, 135
Consumer Price Index 106
Cooley, Alan 113
Coombs, H.C. ('Nugget') 1, 45, 87–88, 138
Crown Prince of Tonga 130
Curtin, John 2, 9, 50
Curtis, W.J. 27
Cyclone *Tracy* (*see under* Darwin)

Daily Telegraph (*see under* Media)
Daly, Thomas 33
Darwin 132;
    Cyclone *Tracy* 90–91, 116
Defence Act 1915 (*see under* Legislation)
Defence Budget 21, 22–24, 27, 34, 36, 38, 42, 64–65, 67, 80, 88–89, 97, 107–108
Defence Council (Australia) 99, 107

Defence Force Ombudsman 85
Defence Reorganisation Act 1976 (*see under* Legislation)
Defence Reorganisation Bill (*see under* Legislation)
Defence Review (1972): 40–41, 44–45, 80, 90
Defence Science 28, 52, 68, 117–18, 128, 135
Defence Science and Technology Organisation (DSTO) 118
Delta Air Lines 115
Denmark 85
Department of Labour (Australia) 22
Department of External Affairs (Australia) (later Department of Foreign Affairs) 1–3, 5, 7–8, 10–14, 17–20, 26, 30, 34–37, 41, 47(*n*10), 70, 76, 86, 92–93, 96, 108, 110, 130–35, 137–38
(*see also* Department of Foreign Affairs))
Department of Foreign Affairs (Australia) (formerly Department of External Affairs and now Department of Foreign Affairs and Trade) 20–21, 36–37, 40, 43, 46, 74, 81–82, 86, 95, 106, 109–110, 113, 138
(*see also* Department of External Affairs)
Desai, Morarji 122–23
Dibb, Paul 37, 52, 82, 125, 140(*n*8)
Ditchley seminar (*see under* Britain)
Dovers, Bill 51
Drake-Brockman, Tom 25
Dulles, John Foster 131
Dunnett, 'Ned' 115
Duntroon (*see* Royal Military College of Australia, Duntroon)
Dutch New Guinea 6, 10
(*see also* Papua New Guinea)
Dwyer, Eric 50–51
Dyer, Brigadier 123

Eastman, Alan 11
Eden, Anthony 132
Egypt:
    Cairo 6
Enfield, John 28
European Economic Commission 112
Evatt, Dr D.V. 1–2, 4, 70, 131, 133, 137

F-111 strategic bomber (*see under* General Dynamics)
Fabian Society (of Victoria) 91
Facilities (defence/military in Australia): 41–42, 49–51, 70, 76, 80, 82, 89, 104, 124;
    Facilities Division 100

(*see also* Joint Defence Space Communications Facility)
(*see also* Joint Defence Space Research Facility)
Fairbairn, David 35–36, 42–43, 45–46, 52, 90, 133
Fairfax (*see under* Media)
Fairhall, Allen 21–22, 24, 27, 37, 61, 65–66, 110
Farrands, John Laws 37, 50–51, 68, 71, 118, 127–29
Federal Constitution (Australia) (*see under* Constitutionality)
Federal Republic of Germany, (as former 'West Germany') 43, 85, 112
(*see also* Second World War)
Fiji 99, 129–30
Fink, Tom 118
First World War 102
Fishing 34, 37, 114–15
Five Year Defence Rolling Program 23
'fortress Australia', concept of 35, 48(*n*23, 24)
'forward defence', concept of 35, 38, 45, 48(*n*23, 24), 103
France 87, 105–106, 112;
  Paris 6
Fraser, Malcolm 1, 15, 19–25, 27, 29–34, 47(*n*2, 19), 50, 58, 64, 66, 77, 82, 85, 90, 94, 97, 99, 102–105, 107, 109, 111–17, 120, 122, 124–25, 129, 131, 133, 137, 139, 140(*n*1, 5);
  Nareen, property at, of, 111
Fremantle 44
Freeth, Gordon 19
Furlonger, Robert 11, 32, 80

Garden Island 44–45
Gardner, Ava 114
General Dynamics:
  F-111 strategic bomber 20, 29–30
Germany (*see* Federal Republic of Germany)
Gorton, John 1, 15, 19–20, 29, 31–36, 41, 43, 47(*n*2), 48(*n*23), 50, 85, 105, 113, 133–35, 137
Gromyko, Andrei 133
Green, Fred J. 30, 54, 57
Green, Marshall 83
Gross Domestic Product (GDP) 97

Haig, Alexander 112
Hamer, David 65
Hamilton, R.N. 36, 40

Hancock, Valston 13
Hannah, Colin 13, 30
Hansard 53
Harvard University 114
Hasluck, Paul 2, 8, 13–15, 19, 31, 34, 36, 40, 116, 133, 135
Hassett, Francis 60, 100, 116
Hawke, Bob 71–73, 77, 82, 136, 140(*n*1)
Hay, David 11, 31
Hayden, Bill 77
Hicks, Edwin 9, 17, 20, 125
Hilton Hotel (*see under* Sydney)
HMAS *Brisbane* (*see under* Royal Australian Navy)
HMAS *Canberra* (*see under* Royal Australian Navy)
HMAS *Parramatta* (*see under* Royal Australian Navy)
Holsworthy 123
Hope, Robert 92–93, 108;
  Hope Report 93, 95, 111;
  Royal Commission on Intelligence 92, 99, 108
Horne, Donald 40, 48(*n*24)
Hotel Canberra 137
House of Representatives (Australia) 43, 49, 65, 113

Imperial Defence College (*see under* Britain)
Imperial Service Club (Sydney) 35, 48(*n*23)
India 15–17, 19–20, 29, 123, 133;
  Lok Sabha 15;
  New Delhi 14–15, 17, 20, 34, 78, 119, 122;
  Punjab 78, 123
Indian Ocean 21, 103–105, 125
Indonesia 6, 10, 12–14, 27, 37, 39, 40, 42, 47(*n*10), 85;
  Partai Komunis Indonesia (PKI) in 10

Japan 38, 56, 83, 104, 131;
  Tokyo 19–20, 47(*n*13)
Jenkins, Roy 112
Jockel, Gordon 37, 52, 80–81
Joint Defence Space Communications Facility 49, 69–75
Joint Defence Space Research Facility 49, 69–75, 94–95, 129
Joint Intelligence Bureau 10
Joint Intelligence Committee 7, 10
Joint Intelligence Organisation (JIO) 32, 37, 80–81, 94, 110–12, 117
Joint Military Staff 51

Joint Planning Committee 8
Journalism (*see under* Media)

Kai-shek, Chiang 3, 5
Kashmir 15
Keating, Paul 43
Kelly, Paul 97
Kennedy, John Fitzgerald 30, 83
Kerr, John Robert 31, 127–29
Killen, James 25, 77, 82, 87, 90, 98(*n*7), 99, 103, 106–108, 111, 121, 124, 140(*n*6)
Kirk, Norman 52
Kissinger, Henry 83
'Koonaroo' 115–17
Korean War 131
Kumaramangalam, General 16

Laird, Melvin 30
Landau, Sam 54, 57, 86
Legislation 28, 50, 54, 59–60, 67, 85, 89, 97, 99;
   Audit Act 1901 57–58;
   Defence Act 1915 58, 99;
   Defence Reorganisation Act 1976 60;
   Defence Reorganisation Bill 97;
   Public Service Act 1922 58
Lloyd, Clem 68, 77–79, 98(*n*6)
Lockheed Corporation:
   C-130 *Hercules* 39
Lok Sabha (*see under* India)
London (*see under* Britain)
Lyneham, Paul 129

MacArthur, Douglas 4
MacDonald, Arthur L. 61, 63, 68, 121–22
Macmillan, Harold 54–55
Malaya 5, 11–12, 21, 105, 139
   (*see also* Malaysia)
Malaysia 10, 12–14, 27, 39–40, 42, 45, 78, 81;
   Borneo, incorporation of, into 12;
   Sabah, incorporation of, into 12
   (*see also* Malaya)
Mara, Ratu Sir Kamisese 129
Martin, Leslie 31
McBride, Philip 5, 132
McEwen, John 47(*n*9), 133
McMahon, William 15, 20–21, 34–36, 43, 45–46, 49–50, 99, 133
McNamara, Robert 23, 28
McNeill, Ian 26
McNicoll, Alan 10

Media 29, 46, 79, 97, 105, 123;
   Age 65;
   Australian Broadcasting Corporation (ABC) 129;
   Bulletin 40, 62, 113;
   Canberra Times 79;
   Daily Telegraph 32;
   Fairfax 128–29;
   Journalism 129;
   National Times 128–29
Menon, Krishna 15
Menzies, Robert 4, 8–9, 11–12, 14–15, 19, 21, 25–27, 40, 50, 52–53, 56, 78, 80, 131–35, 137
Middle East 2, 4, 9, 93, 132, 139
Millar, T.B. (Tom) 64, 81
Ministerial Defence Conference 79
Missiles 69, 71, 73, 77, 108, 117;
   SS-20 *Sabre* missile 105;
   Tartar missile 44
Mornington Peninsula 39
Morrison, William 82, 90, 92, 95–97, 98(*n*7), 128
Morshead, Leslie 23;
   Morshead Committee 25, 52
Moscow (*see under* Soviet Union)
Moten, John 28
Myers, Rupert 121

Nareen (*see under* Fraser, Malcolm)
Nasser, Gamal Abdel 132
National Capital Planning Authority 121
National Intelligence Committee (NIC) 32, 94, 110
National Times (*see under* Media)
Natural Disasters Organisation (NDO) 85, 90
Navy, Australian (*see* Royal Australian Navy)
Nehru, Jawaharlal 15
New Delhi (*see under* India)
New York (*see under* United States)
New Zealand 10, 52, 115
Newspapers (*see* Media)
Nixon, Richard 21, 83, 114
Non-Aligned Movement 15
North Atlantic Treaty Organization (NATO) 11, 105
North Korea 3–4, 138
North West Cape Naval Communications Station (*see under* United States)
Nuclear 71–72, 76;
   balance 73, 80, 95, 103;

energy 84, 112;
forces 10, 69, 71–72, 77;
powered vessels 84;
test ban 71;
Test Ban Treaty 75;
weapons 73, 84
Nurrungar (*see* Joint Defence Space Communications Facility)

Office of National Assessments (ONA) 112
O'Neill, Robert 3

Pacific Islands Regiment 31
Pacific Ocean 21, 44, 104
Packard, David 74
Pakistan 15–16, 119
Papua New Guinea 42
  (*see also* Dutch New Guinea)
Paris (*see under* France)
Parkinson, Nicholas 115
Parliamentary Public Works Committee 122
Partai Komunis Indonesia (PKI) (*see under* Indonesia)
Peacock, Andrew 25, 103, 105
Peck, Gregory 114
Pentagon (*see under* United States)
People's Republic of China 3–5, 11, 14, 16, 104, 131, 138;
  Beijing 3
Petrov, Evdokia 132
Pilger, John 128–29
Pine Gap (*see* Joint Defence Space Research Facility)
Pinochet, Augusto 94
Pinwill, William 128–29
Plimsoll, James 4, 15, 19–20
Poyser, Gordon 10
Press (*see* Media)
Princess Anne, Princess Royal, The 130
Pritchett, W.B. 37, 103, 106
Privileges Committee 130
Public Service (Australia) 1–2, 10, 24, 26–28, 60, 69, 74, 86–87, 89, 100–101, 113, 126, 129–30, 133–36, 138
Public Service Act 1922 (*see under* Legislation)
Public Service Board (Australia) 51, 85, 113
Punjab (*see under* India)

Rand Corporation 23
Reid, Alan 79
Remembrance Day service 97
Rhee, Syngman 20

Rice, Walter 75
Rickover, Hyman G. 84
RMS *Queen Mary* (*see under* Britain)
Rowell, Sydney 7
Roy Milne Memorial Lecture 23, 125
Royal Australian Air Force 16, 24–25, 29–30, 36–37, 39, 41–42, 55, 59–60, 63, 65, 67, 82, 85, 90, 102, 105, 108, 120;
  Chief of Air Staff 30, 62, 101
  (*see also* Boeing)
Royal Australian Navy 7, 18, 24–25, 30, 39, 41–42, 44–45, 54–56, 59–60, 63, 82, 89–90, 97, 99, 101–102, 108, 135, 140(*n*1);
  Chief of Naval Staff 10, 56, 62, 116;
  HMAS *Brisbane* 44;
  HMAS *Canberra* 124;
  HMAS *Parramatta* 44
Royal College of Defence Studies (*see under* Britain)
Royal Military Academy Sandhurst (*see under* Britain)
Royal Military College of Australia, Duntroon 85, 119–20
Rusk, Dean 12–13, 40
Russia 105
  (*see also* Soviet Union)

Saab:
  Viggen (Thunderbolt) aircraft 85
Sabah (*see under* Malaysia)
Saigon (*see under* Vietnam)
Salisbury 117
Sandhurst (*see under* Britain)
Sandys, Duncan 54
Savoy Hotel (*see under* Britain)
Scherger, Frederick 39
Schlesinger, James 83–84
Schmidt, Helmut 43
Seattle (*see under* United States)
Second World War 5, 19, 25, 44, 61, 91, 109, 132, 134, 139
Senate (Australian) 49, 64, 97, 106
Service Boards 28, 51, 54, 56, 58–59, 61–64, 86, 139
Service Chiefs 7–9, 25, 27, 35, 37–38, 43, 54, 57–59, 64, 80, 100, 138
Shackley, Ted 95, 128
Shann, Keith 113
Shedden, Frederick 2–3, 7–9, 17, 125
Ships 22, 24, 39, 60, 80, 86, 108, 124, 127
  (*see also* Nuclear)
Shute, Nevil 114

Singapore 5, 11, 21, 27, 35, 45, 70, 74, 78, 81
Singleton 44
Smith, Victor 32, 52,57, 67
Snedden, Billy 70
South Head (Sydney) 44
South Korea 3
Southeast Asia 3–6, 13–14, 21, 37, 41–43, 77, 104
   (*see also* Association of Southeast Asian Nations (ASEAN))
Southeast Asia Treaty Organisation (SEATO) 10, 13
Soviet Union 3, 10–11, 15–16, 43, 50, 69, 72, 74, 76–77, 88, 94, 96, 103–106, 112–13;
   Moscow 2, 15, 96, 132
   (*see also* Russia)
Spender, Percy C. 2–6, 21, 131–33
SS-20 *Sabre* missile (*see under* Missiles)
Stephen, Ninian 116
Stevenson, David 116
Stone, John 88
Strategic and Defence Studies Centre (SDSC) (*see under* Australian National University, The)
Strategic Basis of Australian Defence Policy paper 11, 82
Strategic Guidance paper 82
Stretton, Alan 90–91, 98(*n*9)
Suez Canal crisis 132
Sukarno, President 10, 12, 14, 16, 39
Supply Department 50, 68, 118, 135
Sweden 85
   (*see also* Barnard, Lance)
Sydney 2, 44, 95–96, 114, 123;
   Hilton Hotel in 122
Synnot, Anthony 68, 91

Tange Report 53, 59
Tartar missile (*see under* Missiles)
Television (*see* Media)
Test Ban Treaty (*see under* Nuclear)
Tokyo (*see under* Japan)
Toohey, Brian 68, 76, 128–29
Townley, Athol 12
Treasury (Australia) 1, 23, 27–28, 31, 43, 51, 88, 97, 100
Truman, Harry S. 4

United Kingdom (*see* Britain)
United Nations 1–3, 15, 31, 134, 138;
   United Nations Security Council 3, 133

United Nations Security Council (*see under* United Nations)
United States 3–6, 9–13, 15, 17, 20–21, 29–30, 37, 39–41, 45, 49–51, 62, 68–79, 82–88, 90–91, 94–97, 103, 105–106, 113–14, 117, 128–29, 131–32, 134, 138–39;
   Air Force 29–30;
   Boston 114;
   Central Intelligence Agency (CIA) 94–95, 128;
   Coast Guard 96;
   Congress 6, 17, 72, 75, 86;
      Armed Services Committee of 45;
   Department of State 6;
   North West Cape Naval Communications Station 13, 76–77, 83–85;
   Navy 13, 76, 84;
   New York 1–2, 4, 114;
   Pentagon 23, 30, 83, 86, 96, 105–106;
   Seattle 124;
   Washington 2, 4, 6–7, 12, 14, 19, 30, 34, 40, 47(*n*13), 71, 83, 93, 95, 114–15, 128;
   White House 45, 114
University of Adelaide 121
University of New South Wales 118, 121–22;
   Australian Defence Force Academy (ADFA), creation of, within 31, 45, 99, 119, 121–22, 124, 127
University of Western Australia 103

Victoria Barracks 44
Vietnam 6, 14–15, 17, 24, 27, 29, 32, 35–36, 41–42, 54, 104, 116–17, 139;
   Saigon 17, 32
Viggen (Thunderbolt) aircraft (*see under* Saab)
Vyshinsky, Andrei 6

Waller, Keith 19–20
Washington (*see under* United States)
Watt, Alan S. 2–3, 6
Wellington Staff College 16
White, Bruce 50, 54, 55–57
White, Frederick 37
White, Thomas 19
White House (*see under* United States)
Whitlam, Gough 15, 43, 49–50, 52, 55, 69–72, 74, 78–79, 83, 86–87, 89, 91–96, 106, 109, 113–14, 128–29, 133, 135, 137
Williamstown Dockyard 99
Wilson, Roland 1
Wilton, John 26

Woodward, Albert Edward 51
Woomera 99, 117, 124
    (*see also* Joint Defence Space
    Communications Facility)
Wran, Neville 122
Wrigley, Allan 129

Yaouk Valley (*see* 'Koonaroo')
Yeend, Geoffrey 122–23

Zetland 45
Zumwalt, Elmo R. 84

www.ingramcontent.com/pod-product-compliance
Lightning Source LLC
Chambersburg PA
CBHW060947170426
43197CB00031B/2986